SLIP away From Harm: Save at Risk & Disabled Lives via Police Harmony

Thad Hughes

Contents

PREFACE

Make no mistake about it, this is not a book about hate, intolerance, or disrespect for law enforcement. Rather, "SLIP" is intended to serve as an essential part of an awareness program for young people who might be on a path that is going to cause them to collide head-on with any police officer who is prone to use deadly force as the primary policing tool.

Historically speaking, two years after the signing of the U.S. Constitution in June 1789, James Madison of Virginia who later became our fourth president proposed 12 amendments, 10 of which became known as the Bill of Rights. The purpose was to restrict governments, rather than individuals and private groups. This was done at the insistence of those who feared a strong central government. Having said that, this is a book about proper trust and mutual respect and it tries to hammer home an ultimate truth, that is; no one is above or exempt from the protections of the Constitutional

Bill of Rights. That includes police officers. A Bill of Rights is what the people are entitled to against every government on earth, Thomas Jefferson, 1787.

Another purpose of this book is to attract attention, both positive and negative, to the widespread problems of police excessive force, particularly the shooting of people that are not armed with guns. The men of our First Congress… knew that whatever form it may assume, the government is potentially as dangerous a thing as it is a necessary one, U.S. Supreme Court Chief Justice Earl Warren.

Last but not least, the main purpose of this book is to promote self-preservation via a four word, common sense message: "Always cooperate, never resist," whenever law enforcement officers are questioning or arresting. If we follow those four words, police officers will probably not kill us. In other words, Stop and Listen to the Instructions of the Police (SLIP). Please don't just practice the SLIP philosophy for your own safety, but rather, tell others who need to hear it from you.

1 Deeper than Racism

A database of The Guardian newspaper reported that in 2016, the police killed 1092 people. Per million, the data breaks down as follows:

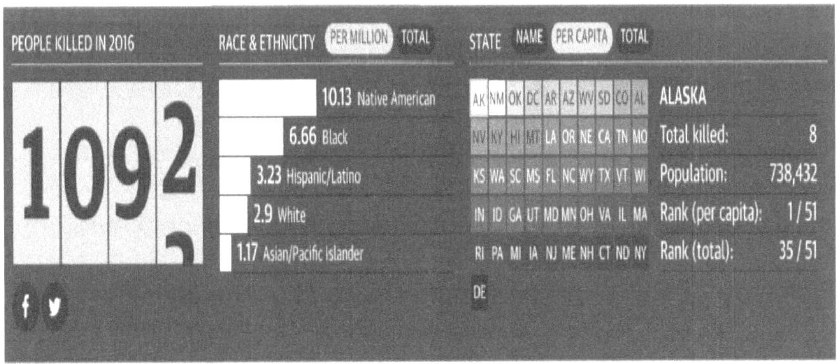

By comparison, in 2015, the police killed a total of 1,146 people, altogether. Per million, the data breaks down as follows:

2.9 white people killed, 6.66 black people, 3.23 Latino/Hispanic, 10.13 Native Americans, and 1.17 Asians/Pacific Islanders. Believe it or not, those numbers are down categorically from 2015, with one exception. The exception is, the percentage of Native Americans killed by the police skyrocketed in 2016.

2.95 white people killed, 7.69 black people, 3.45 Latino/Hispanic, 5.49 Native Americans, and 1.34 Asians/Pacific Islanders. I urge you to read The Guardian's report on people killed by the police. You will find that The Guardian's categorized collection of data on police killings is as good as any. Simply go to https://www.theguardian.com/us-news/ng-interactive/2015/jun/01/the-counted-police-killings-us-database. Do not forget to make use of the convenient state by state analytical tool that is provided within the link.

Another key issue which calls for racial debate is whether or not racial profiling really exist. According to an independent study conducted by SDSU, racial profiling remains an issue affecting blacks and Hispanics when stopped by the San Diego police. The October 2016 released study, was a two year study that examined 259,000 traffic stops conducted from 2014 to 2015. Curiously, blacks and

Hispanics, though, more often subjected to deeper questions and search than whites, the police found, whites possessed more contrabands than blacks and Hispanics.

There are numerous studies, such as the above mentioned SDSU study, which show similar results. Still, some skeptics raise the question, does racism matter, in the grand scheme of police relations in America? Yes, of course, racism matters, but if we fix the way people relate to the police, that can be the tide that raises all ships. Besides, if America has shown us one thing in the last two years, it is this, the more one side talks about racial problems, the more the other side digs in its hills and sticks its fingers in its ears to block out all dialogue. There is a win-win way to fix the problem of people dying by the police. I suggest a way, quite frankly, all good and decent people will agree with because good police don't want to kill people and they don't want to be vilified and seen as bad people because they are good.

The solution to the problem of the police having to resort to using deadly force is a three prong educational approach. 1) Educate children specifically about the importance of listening to and doing what the police tells us to do. 2) Create hiring and training policies with enough teeth to demand and enforce a culture of zero tolerance for excessive force and corruption. 3) Educate the public to remove the negative stigma of soft on crime when people provide strict follow up on citizen complaints and for holding police officers accountable from the top, down to the bottom ranks.

I am the father of a son who turned 9-years-old in December 2017. The subject of police and community relations is nearer and dearer to my heart than ever. I am concerned about the future, and this writing reflects the beginning of me trying to make a difference. For example, we need to look closely at the June 19, 2018 police shooting of the unarmed 17-year-old, Antwon Rose, by East Pittsburg Police Officer Michael Rosfeld. Clearly, we have much to do differently.

Of this I know, many people are convinced, racial discrimination by the police is the culprit which drives bad public and police relations. I say, fix the problem of excessive force, and greatly reduce the use of deadly force. Then, we will see a vast majority of all headline grabbing, highly controversial, negative police issues disappear. My hypothesis is, excessive use of deadly force is the tide that raises and lowers all ships. Therefore, it is the excessive use of deadly force which is causing historically poor police and community relations.

Back in 2000, I wrote a book about police mistrust. Due to my knee jerk state of mind, back then, I named that book, "201 Reasons Not to Trust Police--The Crooked Ones." I said my piece, and then, I moved on. I thought those dark, disappointing episodes were over and done. I was wrong, though, the dreary disasters of police mistrust never go away. Police mistrust is an unfortunate way of life, these days, in America.

The ugly saga of so many lives being taken in America by citizens, killing police officers, and the police killing citizens, caused me to go back and do some deep soul searching on the topic. I am extremely proud of how much my attitude and views on the subject of policing have grown in positive ways, by comparison, to how I felt back in 2000.

In my naiveté, I theorized back in 2000: "Surely racism is the smoking gun that triggers the ignorant devil, which we know as police mistrust in America." As I sit here today, nearly 20 years later, I know that such theories, though, well intentioned and often repeated, are gross oversimplifications of a complex problem. The facts, simply do not bear out a direct single handed cause and effect relationship. To say that the cause of lousy police conflict resolutions in America, is racism, just because it is low hanging fruit, is irresponsible and serves to divide our country along racial lines in the worst of ways. But are people choosing to go after that low hanging fruit, purely without merit? The answer is no.

The fact that racism exists in all human beings is undeniable, police officers, not excluded. Just Google the story of a former skinhead named, Christian Picciolini. There he reveals some dirty details about a popular career path that young racists are encouraged to pursue—first go to the military to receive training, and then join law enforcement. Although, it was refreshing to hear an insider confess those words on camera during a 60 Minutes interview, I figured that out for myself a long time ago.

To the naked and unlearned eye, racism can appear to be the only driving mechanism for excessive force in certain communities. Based on the appearance of racism, I used to subscribe to the racism theory, myself. Then, I sat down and did a little research on the matter. The unpleasant nature of the overall alarming rate of the deadly police force used against people of all races, caused me to conclude, we should abstain from the knee jerk reaction of automatically defaulting to racism as the key trigger, each time a police Involved death occurs in certain communities.

According to thinkprogress.org.

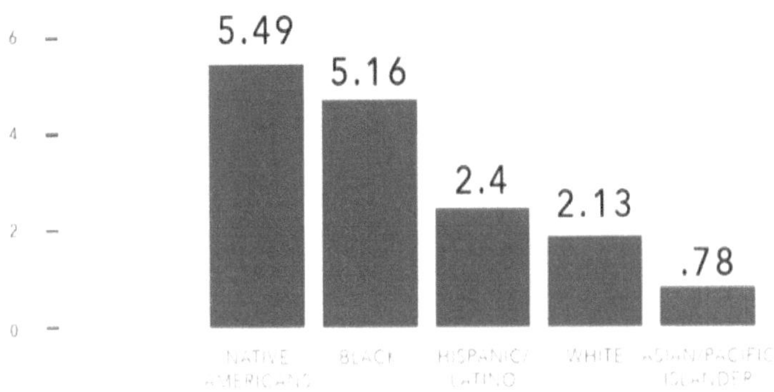

There you'll see how many people the police killed in 2016.

Another excellent resource is http://killedbypolice.net. On the latter website you can see, day by day, the number of people killed by the police, as well as, their race, age and gender.

December 31st - January 1st, 2016 **(1156)**

# since Jan 1st '16	St.	g/r	Name, Age	*	KBP link (plus roughly 100,000 follow-ups)
					December (90)
(1156) December 31, 2016	FL	M/W	Daniel Ralph Daily, 34	G	facebook.com/permalink.php?story_fbid=1228132063918984&id=956901834375343
(1155) December 31, 2016	MN	M/W	Chase Anthony Tuseth, 33	G	facebook.com/permalink.php?story_fbid=1227946070604250&id=956901834375343
(1154) December 31, 2016	PA	M/W	Jason Michael Robison, 32	G	facebook.com/permalink.php?story_fbid=1227824223949768&id=956901834375343
(1153) December 31, 2016	FL	M/W	Ricky Kevin Whidden, 46	G	facebook.com/permalink.php?story_fbid=1227802997285224&id=956901834375343
(1152) December 31, 2016	CA	M	Donald Joseph Hill, 30	R	facebook.com/KilledByPolice/posts/1480062532021879
(1151) December 30, 2016	FL	M/B	Jamar Rollins, 21	G	facebook.com/permalink.php?story_fbid=1227666803965510&id=956901834375343
(1150) December 30, 2016	AZ	M/W	Dustin Lee Selby, 31	G	facebook.com/permalink.php?story_fbid=1227145824017608&id=956901834375343
(1149) December 29, 2016	FL	M/W	John Sellinger, 34	TRC	facebook.com/permalink.php?story_fbid=1227155767349947&id=956901834375343
December 29, 2016	WI	F/W	Samantha Norris	V	facebook.com/KilledByPolice/posts/1577086598986138
(1148) December 28, 2016	MD	M/B	James L. Rich II, 52	G	facebook.com/permalink.php?story_fbid=1226064014125789&id=956901834375343
(1147) December 28, 2016	TN	M/W	Christopher Blake Tucker, 28	G	facebook.com/permalink.php?story_fbid=1226022147463309&id=956901834375343
December 28, 2016	FL	M/B	Nathan Howard Hamilton, 39	TR	facebook.com/permalink.php?story_fbid=1225298234202367&id=956901834375343
(1146) December 27, 2016	SD	M/I	Julio Joseph Bald Eagle, 19	G	facebook.com/permalink.php?story_fbid=1226407337424790&id=956901834375343
(1145) December 27, 2016	KY	M/W	David Carver, 34	G	facebook.com/permalink.php?story_fbid=1225356254196565&id=956901834375343
(1144) December 27, 2016	TX	M/W	Jake Childers, 36	G	facebook.com/permalink.php?story_fbid=1225264117539112&id=956901834375343
(1143) December 27, 2016	IL	M	Alfonso D. Lopez, 41	G	facebook.com/permalink.php?story_fbid=1225234614208729&id=956901834375343
(1142) December 27, 2016	TX	F/W	Judy Boardman Hundley, 71	G	facebook.com/permalink.php?story_fbid=1224693984262792&id=956901834375343
(1141) December 27, 2016	CA	M/W	Dustin Kirk, 35	G	facebook.com/permalink.php?story_fbid=1224614830937374&id=956901834375343
(1140) December 25, 2016	OR	M/W	James Tylka, 30	G	facebook.com/permalink.php?story_fbid=1223809961017861&id=956901834375343
(1139) December 25, 2016	AR	M	Joseph Garcia, 33	G	facebook.com/permalink.php?story_fbid=1223261361072721&id=956901834375343
(1138) December 25, 2016	DC	M/B	Gerald Javon Hall, 29	G	facebook.com/permalink.php?story_fbid=1223254784406712&id=956901834375343
(1137) December 25, 2016	FL	M/W	Michael Alan Altice, 61	G	facebook.com/permalink.php?story_fbid=1223129154419275&id=956901834375343
(1136) December 24, 2016	TX	M/W	Jesse Andrew DeBusk, 38	R	facebook.com/permalink.php?story_fbid=1224431967622327&id=956901834375343
(1135) December 24, 2016	CA	M/A	Zhonghua Li, 48	G	facebook.com/permalink.php?story_fbid=1222555697809954&id=956901834375343

Most people are surprised by the eye popping number of white people being killed by police on a consistent basis. As a black man, I was equally shocked and appalled. After viewing these two referenced websites, you will come away thinking not so much about why are the police taking so many black lives, but rather why are the police taking so many lives, period?

Make no mistake, though, facts show one black male is likely to be killed by the police per every 21 white males. Racism is a problem that merits high concern, but it is not the key trigger of poor police conflict resolution in America. Based upon the dead body count, which grows higher by the day, due to people dying at the hands of police officers, I'd say that excessive force and outdated training is the real culprit.

Face it, if our dumpster fire, which we call, police conflict resolution, could be summed up as "a racial problem in America," how do we account for the secrecy of blacks and non-racist officers in the police forces? Don't you think, if race relations are so poor within law enforcement that white police are going around killing black men for pleasure, black officers and good officers of various races would be whistle blowing at a skyrocketing rate?

For my money, we'd be more productive to focus our critiques on law enforcement weeding out, and not hiring people who are too nervous or cowardly, and those who cannot handle the pressures of the job.

Scientific studies show, "When human beings are saveof negative emotions, like anger, illness, anxiety, worries, fear, hatred, insecurity, etc. The manifestation of such innate human reactions leads to decreased IQ, lack of judgment and self-control, and a narrower scope of consciousness. The culmination of all those natural physiological body changes causes people to subsequently experience a common sense collapse."

That scientific observation is relevant because, at the time of physical confrontation, whether against the police or by the police, people who die from violence fail to grasp the gravity of the situation. Instead, both sides attempt to proceed as though they are dealing with rational individuals who are operating under self-control.

In reality, all people, whether police officers or not, whose demeanor demonstrates negative emotions are the persons who should be treated with caution and higher level people skills. Think of it this way, when you are adversely confronted by a negative person, if you are psychologically in a positive place before you meet them, don't allow yourself to be led astray by their negative energy.

Rather, use your intelligence and wisdom to redirect people's negative energy by leading them in a positive direction, by "Non-action." Such was one of the main philosophical ideas of Lao Tzu, the Daoism founder. "There is nothing undone when we do nothing." Master Lao remarked. Non-action here means we do not act intelligently; we act like a listening child who is showing no threat to our opposition. Thus, we should talk only when asked to. Never talk to defend. Because our silence and acting gentle is the weapon, and positively speaking, is the tool to heal the world, one at a time.

Let me call your attention to an old American psychological test. The psychologist asked a tough guy and an old man to cross streets. Only 50% of the cars stopped for the tough guy. However, 100% of the cars stopped for the old man, and those who stopped were happy because they had done a good deed. So imagine if we were an old man or a small child, would the police treat us differently? Yes, they would, because they would feel less threat than they would feel when dealing with big tall males. The moral of the story is, if we look strong, we are at higher risk.

For the sake of self-preservation, we need to demonstrate via behavior to the police that we are only tough on the surface but we are polite and gentle inside. Also, show that we are positive thinking people who are not easily led by other people's negative emotions. Actions speak louder than voice.

Be wise: talk with respect and remorse about what you are being accused of by the police. Do not argue or shout at the police even if they are shouting at you. Arguing and shouting at police officers are triggers for escalation of violence, which is likely to end with you getting shot and killed. Your death can lead to retaliation against the police, which likely results in random police officers being shot and killed. And of course, the vicious cycle continues, but in the end, nobody wins. The only thing violence in those situations does is create more mistrust and violence in the world.

By acting smart and saving our own lives, we can heal the world, one at a time. After all, if we save our own life, people who love us dearly, do not suffer from living through the grief, committing suicide, or having their quality of life and health drastically affected by our untimely death.

Imagine if Jesus, Socrates, Confucius or Lao Tzu was stopped by a police officer. How would they react? I think you know the answer already. That's why Lao Tzu stated, "The wisest look the most foolish; the gentle outlast the strong; the obscure outlast the obvious!" A big tree looks strong standing, while a blade of grass looks gentle, but it is the tree with its roots that is taken away by the storm, not the grass, which is only bent down by the storm. This teaches us that anyone showing toughness on the surface, like the police, is showing us they are very insecure inside and will easily lose self-control at any time; and thus we must act "foolish", gentle and obscure in order to achieve a successful relationship. Characteristically speaking, such police are the Yang on the outside and Yin on the inside.

To be in accord with the Dao, we have to be a Yin person on the outside, while at the sametime, we must be a Yang person on the inside. This means we should act "weak", polite and gentle while maintaining firm and positive to our beliefs that we are the strongest and most positive compared to our adversaries.

We should believe that we are the masters of the situations which we encounter, and capable of providing leadership to a much calmer state. This state of mind is necessary for creating a win-win outcome, which is parallel to the outcome depicted in this universally harmonious Tai Chi diagram, which teaches us that Yin and Yang are the components of everything in the universe. A woman is a combination of Yin and Yang, and a man is composed of Yang and Yin. And the world is a combination of Yin and Yang with the sky/heaven up high and the earth down below. There would be no lives if the world only had earth but no sky, and there would be no lives if there were only men or only women.

The Tai Chi diagram symbol represents the fact that we can transform the Qi/energy between the irrational person and us into a successful relationship. When viewed through unwise eyes, if a police officer acts aggressive or rude, he looks like he is solely a Yang person, but through the enlightenment of the Dao philosophy, we know that everything is both Yin+Yang. The wisdom of the Dao philosophy causes us to perceive and respond to the troubled police officer totally different from that of a typical knee jerk reaction. Through the Dao, we can see such a troubled police officer's Yin while others cannot see it. We know that the officer's Yin is manifesting itself through various behaviors, such as, the police officer feels insecure and helpless. He suffers from loss of rationality which causes him to operate his life on the edge and make all the wrong decisions while psychologically he's begging for a positive redirect. Now we see this as an opportunity to help another human being who is in need. Why? Because we see an opportunity to apply the art of war and perhaps bring about the Yin/Yang transformation, so that we can first save our own life and then maybe save the life of the police officer afterwards by sparing him legal troubles or physical violence. This creates a win-win situation.

To handle such situations highlighted above in a contrary manner will prevent us from achieving a win-win situation. Instead, the opposite is true. When we go against the principles of the Dao, we create chaos. Thereby, lives are lost on a consistent basis due to people failing to accept this simple reality.

2 **What Went Wrong?**

Throughout this book, you will see the acronym SLIP, as well as the phrase SLIP Away from Harm, used over and over again. In fact, Chapters Three and Four of this book gives readers a thorough explanation of everything that SLIP and SLIP Away from Harm is all about. As for now, let's suffice it to say, SLIP stands for, "Stop and Listen to Instructions of the Police." SLIP Away from Harm, is a slogan that makes SLIP a memorable catchphrase. SLIP is a method used for teaching people, as young as elementary school age, how to conduct themselves responsibly while maintaining harmony, and staying safe when dealing with police officers.

SLIP is a win-win concept because it saves lives of citizens and it makes the jobs of police officers easier and safer. So why not give SLIP a try? Chapters Three and Four of this book are dedicated to teaching how, what, and why SLIP is the right solution for healing community and police relations in America today.

But for now, I have a question for you. Have you ever watched a man die? Not talking about the make belief stuff you can see in movies, on TV, and in video games.

Just like video games, the movie and TV version of death is scripted art that is done for entertainment value. I mean, have you ever watched a man die? Be forewarned, though, if you have the stomach for it, I urge you to log on http://photographyisnotacrime.com and see what police officers are up against out there and what risk people take every time they choose not to SLIP Away from Harm. The way I see it, we need to embrace SLIP principals, until and unless, we become wise enough to, "Do to others as we would have them do to us." Luke 6:31

Citizens are violently killing police officers, and police officers violently kill citizens. That is dark and dreary, but that is, in fact, the reality that we live In now. I received an epiphany from this web link https://photographyisnotacrime.com/2015/12/19/los-angeles-deputy-shoots-partner-blames-suspect-both-kill-suspect-in-retaliation/. I watched a video titled "Los Angeles Deputy Shoots Partner, Blames Suspect; Both Kills Suspect in Retaliation."

Los Angeles Deputy Shoots Partner, Blames Suspect; Both Kill Suspect in Retaliation

Here you will see video footage that will change your life forever. That I guarantee. If you are like most people, this will be your first time watching a real life nightmare unfold from start to finish right before your very eyes. Burned into my brain forever are the final words of the dying victim, "I'm dying!" He said, fading away.

I sat and watched that particular incident of two police officers attempting to make an arrest of a young man who resisted arrest.

One thing led to another, and the result was, both police officers fired multiple shots into the living body of the young man at point blank range. Then, little by little, the young man struggled less and less, and his energetic outcries waned more and more silent—then nothing—no more movement and complete silence. And just like that, the young man was gone.

Just for a moment, I realized that the young man, dying there with his face down on the pavement was somebody's son. Just for a moment, my human nature allowed me to superimpose my son's body in the place of the dying young man. I felt a sniffle in my nose, as the tears attempted to rise-up from distant places of my eyes. My son will know how to SLIP Away from Harm, but that young man did not know, and it resulted in him dying a horrific death. As I reflected in horror, just after I finished watching that tragic video, I remember thinking, I only hope that the victim's mother, father and loved ones never watch this video. Of course, I am sure that everybody who knew the victim and is old enough to watch the video of that savage killing, has watched it.

In hindsight, my thoughts are, how did things deteriorate so far, so fast, in that situation? I don't believe for one moment that the police officers showed up thinking, "Wow, today sure is another beautiful day in Southern CA. Isn't it? Let's go shoot and kill that unarmed young man because that looks like a fun and exciting thing to do." I do not believe that is what happened at all. Having been in the shoes of a police officer before, I feel certain; the officers were thinking and hoping, let's just do our jobs and go over there and arrest this guy and get him off the streets. However, for whatever reason, the young man, seemed hell-bent on not going to jail. That uncooperative behavior, set in motion the wheels of destruction for his family, the police officers, and himself. Although clearly, that young man did not deserve to be killed that way on that day, he should have chosen to SLIP Away from Harm, though. Instead, that young man chose to FLIP Away to Harm. FLIP stands for Failure to Listen to Instructions of the Police.

I chose not to disclose the identity of the victim of the above case before now because I wanted each person who reads his story, for the first time, to be able to imagine that the victim is someone they know and care about on a personal level. For the record, the victim was Noel Enrique Aguilar; he was a 23-year-old, Hispanic male. The young Mr Aguilar's life was cut short by the police on May 26, 2014. Two Los Angeles County Sheriff Deputies fatally shot and killed Mr

Aguilar, just after they chased him for riding a bicycle while wearing

headphones. The tragedy climaxed at around 10 a.m. on a Monday

morning. The day after the unbelievable killing of Mr Aguilar, the

typical headline about the case read in gist, from the Orange County

Register, Mr Noel Enrique Aguilar shoots L.A. County Sheriff Deputy

because he was a known gang member. As a result, he was shot

and killed by the police.

Unknown to the two officers who killed Mr Aguilar, at the time

they killed the victim, high quality video captured all the mind

numbing images and audio of the killing with indisputable clarity. The

video evidence shows one of the two arresting police officers,

drawing his service pistol before apparently accidentally discharging

said firearm. The accidental shot fired by the first partner struck his

partner in the abdomen. Instead of accepting responsibility for his

mistake of shooting his partner--only God knows why--the officer who

fired the accidental shot began blaming Mr Aguilar for shooting his

partner. For anyone watching the video with objective eyes, a

plausible theory is, the officer who fired the shot into his partner's

abdomen tried to cover up his mistake of accidentally shooting his

partner, by blaming Mr Aguilar. Why wouldn't a person who

accidentally shoots someone just own it, though? I guess, only God

knows why.

After coercing Mr Aguilar failed to get him to confess to

having a gun and shooting the police officer, and from not stating out

loud that he did not shoot the police officer, both police officers shot

and killed Mr Aguilar. While the two officers held Mr Aguilar pinned

down with his face on the pavement, one officer shot Mr Aguilar in his

stomach, and his partner shot Mr Aguilar three times in his back.

Coincidentally, a unique twist of irony in this situation of the police

officer mistakenly firing his firearm followed the tragedy. In that, a

recent two years study funded by Los Angeles County showed that

accidental shootings were up 500 percent between 2012 and 2014.

The dramatic increase in accidental shootings likely resulted from to

the Los Angeles Sheriff's Department issuing new Smith & Wesson

M&P 9mm weapons to its police officers. Clearly, several design

flaws exist in the new weapons which are putting both the public and

police officers at risk.

There are three key lessons we should learn from the case of

Mr Aguilar. Lesson One, racial discrimination was not the primary

motivating factor. Mr Aguilar's case is about the obsessive use of deadly police force. The obsessive use of deadly force in Mr Aguilar's case is wrong, sad, disgusting and horrible; yet clearly, the case was not motivated by racial discrimination. The victim was Hispanic, and one of the police officers who brutally shot and killed him was also Hispanic as well. Also, it is important to note, both officers who killed this victim were minorities. Imagine how perceptions would have played out if the victim was black, and the officers were white. Natural reactions to such tragic events lead us to assume; race must be the primary triggering ingredient. The truth is, excessive use of deadly force and too little regard for human life caused this case to end, most horrifically.

Lesson Two, can we please stop already with the absurd notion that all police officers never lie, manipulate evidence, break laws, or otherwise do horrible things. Who created the insanely false narrative that labels people soft on crime, if we have the audacity to say those words out loud? The elephant in the room alert is: police officers are only human, and they sometimes get put in lousy situations, but just like all other professions, police work, attracts good and bad people.

Lesson Three, we must impress upon the youth of our society to SLIP Away from Harm. Maybe SLIP teachings would have made a difference in Mr Aguilar's case; we will never know. I am sure some people who know of his case cannot get over the fact that Mr Aguilar was no choirboy, and in fact, he was far from sainthood. On the other hand, though, Mr Aguilar was a young man with potentially much to offer. After all, people who are far worse off track than he was, have managed to get their lives turned around, and sometimes those people give back to the communities that they previously terrorized by creating and working in programs that help save the futures of at risk young people.

Mr Aguilar's death is a loss that should cause us to look back from a philosophical perspective and ask ourselves: what would wise men say about Mr Aguilar's horrific tragedy? I am reminded that Socrates said, "The only true wisdom is in knowing you know nothing." This means being humble, thus being cautious, should be a primary survival characteristic. This quote by Socrates, share both irony and parallelism with Sun Zi's wisdom in his book *The Art of War*— "If you know the enemy and know yourself, you need not fear the result of a hundred battles. If you know yourself but not the enemy, for every victory gained you will also suffer a defeat. If you know neither the enemy nor yourself, you will succumb in every battle."

These two wise men, Socrates and Sun Zi, taught us that when we meet a volatile person, such as a police officer, in most cases, he is a stranger to us. Therefore, we do not know anything about him; not his personality, level of humanity, temperament, his past, what happened to him just before he met us, nor what happened to him during his childhood, etc. However, we do know that he is carrying a gun, and that is really all we need to know.

Sun Zi said, "Only if we know the enemy and we know ourselves, we can win," but in chance encounters with police officers, we don't know who we are dealing with well enough to compete "in a war" with them, therefore, we ought to be extra cautious.

It would appear, then if we meet an unfamiliar police officer, we would be in Sun Zi's philosophic category of "knowing ourselves, but not the enemy." However, such an encounter runs contrary to "knowing ourselves, but not the enemy," because it puts us in the category of Sun Zi's "we know neither the enemy nor ourselves."

As you process those words of wisdom that I just mentioned, ponder these words now, Socrates said, wise people only think they know nothing. The situation of Mr Aguilar fell under the category of, not knowing one's self or his enemy because his failure to cooperate with the two police officers caused him to become engaged in a physical conflict with them. The rest is history. One of the police officers accidentally shot his partner, Mr Aguilar would have been wise speaking only words necessary to save his own life during that heated moment.

Mr Aguilar's failure to cooperate resulted in his hands being cuffed behind his back while the police officers pinned him, face down, on the pavement. In hindsight, we see that his noncooperation with the police was a bad idea for so many reasons. First, he had not known the police officer's gun would accidentally discharge, striking his partner--I'm guessing, this was the issue that sealed his fate. Second, he had not known anything about the two police officers yet he assumed that they might be rational thinkers.

So what is the correlation between the fact that Mr Aguilar did not know himself and the fact that the gun accidentally discharged? And why is there a relationship between those two seemingly, unrelated variables? The correlation is, we should always be aware that the world is full of uncertainty and unpredictability. No one knows what tomorrow, the next minute, or the next second brings. We should make decisions and conduct ourselves based on the fact that the unknown is very powerful.

Therefore, when faced by volatile people, no matter what title they go by, of course, we do not know what can go wrong, so it behooves us to remain humble and cautious. In the case of Mr Aguilar, only God knew that the police officer's gun would malfunction.

So then, philosophically speaking, what is the key lesson learned from Mr Aguilar's life ending tragedy by the police? We should learn to be humble enough to realize that we actually know nothing. That is to say, when it comes to meeting such volatile people, we know nothing of their past, present, or future. As for knowing ourselves, the great philosophers would say, "We know nothing about our own present or future, therefore, do not assume anything."

Even when we have done nothing wrong, we should not get angry and shout out loud that we are innocent, as Mr Aguilar did. Instead, be patient and we will get our opportunity to speak out and defend ourselves in the right place and right time. In the heat of conflict, generally speaking, people don't believe a stranger's word anyhow. Rather, people judge strangers more so by action, not words. If people sense that you are displaying rudeness, impatience, or disrespect, people tend to tune out the words you say. This takes us back to the philosophy of, "people know nothing." Although people know nothing, they make assumptions, based on first impressions that certain behaviors mean, "this man is a criminal because he does not act gentle, polite and respectful."

Due to knee jerk reactions from people, Confucius said, "When the state goes on the right way, one should be honest in word and in deed. When the state goes on the wrong way, one should be honest in actions, but cautious in the word!" Literally speaking, the state used in this context, means small country, because when

Confucius spoke, China consisted of a few states. There was not a big united China yet.

As for today on a national level, based on face value, the police puts us in a dilemma. Our dilemma is, based on face value, we cannot be sure if the police are on the right way, or the wrong way, so we should assume it is on the wrong way for now. Unfortunately, if we assume the police is on the right way, we might become too confident and lose our lives. That is to say, if we assume our police state is in the wrong way now, we would act more cautiously during our interactions with the police.

This philosophy of reacting wisely to the authority of the state served Confucius well. Although Confucius was a free thinker back when thinking outside the box could get you beheaded, Confucius thrived for many years and died of old age. There were many times, Confucius spoke in the presence of kings and dukes, who were like the police nowadays who held the power to take human life. Confucius knew that like everybody else in the world, he had a huge purpose for being here, so he had to be cautious every step he took.

Using proper caution allows us to keep the breath of life in our bodies so that we can accomplish our soul's goal.

3 SLIP Solutions

SLIP aims to teach people, from early childhood, how to recognize the fundamental importance of stopping what they are doing and giving police officers their undivided attention to detail. Failing to use SLIP concepts is at the heart of 99% of all disasters, wherein there are police related killing of citizens. There are various reasons for the cause and effect relationship between the failure to use SLIP principals, and police related killings. I will discuss the cause and effect relationship of SLIP and police related killings in detail later on in this chapter when I talk about a strategy called SLIP Phase 3.

SLIP gives people a more intelligent default mindset, for overcoming a lack of self-control whenever they interact with the police. More times than not, the outcome for failing to yield to police instructions result in a loss of personal freedoms, at the very least. I can say from my personal experiences over the years; it feels good when the police let you go with a warning, rather than having to pay fines or go to jail. Above all, it is smart to avoid getting beaten or shot by the police, wouldn't you agree?

Let's take a moment and ponder an analogy of art imitating life. In the 2016 animated movie, "Sing", there is a porcupine character who is called, Ash. She is an awesome little rock and roll singer, but whenever her mood becomes upset, sad, or excited, her quills shoot out of her like sharp missiles as they fly through the air indiscriminately. Whoever gets caught in the line of fire receives a heavy dose of Ash's sharp flying needles.

Although that particular bit is hilarious to watch, it is a

stellar teaching metaphor. The problem of someone becoming emotional and causing objects to fly through the air and harm whoever gets in the way is what goes on when a citizen and police interactions go horribly wrong these days.

Scientific findings prove that anyone showing negative emotions can represent a danger to us, but of course, the risks increase when such a person has a gun. To continue our before mentioned porcupine teaching metaphor, sometimes irrational people are already experiencing negative emotions before they approach us, therefore, their quills are already cocked and waiting for one more trigger. If such a person happens to be a police officer, once he meets a person who does not listen or demonstrate sufficient respect, the non-cooperative person will trigger the police officer's quills to shoot out. Under such circumstances, a police officer might be too quick to shoot.

The fact that we all would benefit if we use precaution in each situation involving the presence of police officers, is a no-brainer. We should acknowledge that we might be dealing with an individual who is like a porcupine whose quills are already erected, so we should be much more cautious around them.

The problem is, some people still think it is too much to ask to show respect to anyone who is not respectful to them. While there might be some higher level of dignity in that way of thinking, the reward for winning the war of principle cannot compare to saving our own precious lives, can it? To demand fairness and respect from someone who might shoot us for doing so is not a wise thing to do. If a man lose his life today, how can he demand respect in the future? After all, dead men tell no tale

THE
TEN COMMANDMENTS

I. I AM THE LORD YOUR GOD:
YOU SHALL NOT HAVE
STRANGE GODS BEFORE ME.

II. YOU SHALL NOT TAKE
THE NAME OF THE LORD
YOUR GOD IN VAIN.

III. REMEMBER TO KEEP HOLY
THE LORD'S DAY.

IV. HONOR YOUR FATHER
AND YOUR MOTHER.

V. YOU SHALL NOT KILL

VI. YOU SHALL NOT COMMIT ADULTERY.

VII. YOU SHALL NOT STEAL.

VIII. YOU SHALL NOT BEAR
FALSE WITNESS
AGAINST YOUR NEIGHBOR.

IX. YOU SHALL NOT COVET
YOUR NEIGHBOR'S WIFE.

X. YOU SHALL NOT COVET
YOUR NEIGHBOR'S GOODS.

Furthermore, to show respect in exchange for saving our own lives does not mean that we are showing respect for irrational people who would kill us. In such situations, we are showing respect to the art of war, to the Dao, and to Jesus' wisdom instead. That is the wisdom of self-preservation; the wisdom of "recoil in order to extend," as the idiom says. And in a more earthly sense, we can think of our self-preserving act as showing respect to our parents who gave us precious life and would like nothing more than to see us save ourselves from an untimely death.

After all, we should never forget that the Fourth of the Ten Commandments is: "Honor your father and your mother."

Police Officers are human too. They will not cut you a break if you act like a jerk towards them. Based on my experience of working in law enforcement, as a San Diego County Marshal, it feels good giving a break to good people who will straighten-up, and fly right. More importantly, there is another end of the spectrum, though. As the headline show, all too often these days, when people are not wise enough to use SLIP concepts, life, and death, are at stake.

The question is, when should SLIP concepts be taught to children to have the biggest impact on their lives? Answer: Moms and dads should begin teaching SLIP to children who are approximately 10-years-old, annually on a routinely scheduled basis. Why not make SLIP part of the family's New Year resolution each January, after children are old enough to understand? Think revisiting SLIP each January sounds extreme? Google any one of the high profile cases of victims who died at the hands of the police, dating back to the year, 2000. Then ask yourself, would it have been a good idea to have taught those people to SLIP Away from Harm, every

January?

Theoretically speaking, it is essential to teach SLIP

concepts to age appropriate learners. Younger children do not

need to know the gory details of what happens when police

encounters go horribly wrong. Children just need to know that it

is good to be good, and it is good to treat people well,

especially police officers. Mature people, though, can benefit

from being scared straight by watching raw

downloaded/streamed video of actual police shootings. Of all

the information that exist about police related shootings,

nothing captured my attention, the way, seeing it with my own

eyes, did. Later, this book contains some links to raw video of

police shootings that I recommend, however, several other

such links are easily accessible on the internet.

For schools, however, the first time we need to teach

Children about SLIP is some point before the last year of

elementary school. Therefore, around age 10 is an appropriate

stage of childhood development to introduce SLIP Phase 1

strategy. Because Phase 1 targets little children, focus attention on teaching these basic concepts contained in Reference Chart 1 below.

SLIP Phase 1 Strategy:

Step 1) Always be nice to police officers and greet them with a smile.

Step 2) Police officers keep us safe, so we should trust them.

Step 3) Police officers are very important people, so we must listen to them when they tell us what to do.

For individuals and schools alike, who wish to teach SLIP concepts to children, it is essential to think about always keeping the message simple. Just remember, the volume of research proving that children learn best by doing fun activities are overwhelming. Therefore, teachers of SLIP concepts should creatively use role play and turn taking scenarios.

When teaching SLIP Phase 1 strategy, the adult should act out the role of a police officer, then reverse the roles and give children an opportunity to see how good it feels to have people cooperate with them and listen to what they say when they are police officers. Seize opportunities to call attention to empathy to make children understand how good it makes them feel when people give them due respect and cooperation, while they are serving as police officers.

The second round of introducing SLIP concepts to youngsters should take place during the last year of middle school. Therefore, I recommend implementing SLIP Phase 2 strategy at around age 14-years-old. At 14-years-old, child development is optimum to revisit all the concepts that we taught when children were fourth graders via, SLIP Phase 1. Since Phase 2 targets young teens focus on teaching the basic concepts contained in Reference Chart 2 below.

SLIP Phase 2 Strategy:

Step 1) Now in SLIP Phase 2, expand the teachings of Step 1 to include, always be nice and respectful to the police. Plus, stay calm and cooperate each time you deal with the police.

Step 2) Expand the concepts of SLIP Phase 2, Step 2 to include, the police do not know who you are or what you will do when they meet you. They can only judge you based upon how you act and follow instructions, so you must always act right and do what police officers tell you to do.

Step 3) Expand the concepts of SLIP Phase 2, Step 3 by calling attention to awareness of the consequences which follow not listing to the police and not following instructions of the police. Since there are consequences for failure to SLIP Away from Harm, design lessons that, make sure students know those consequences with crystal clear clarity. Here are three key consequences for failure to SLIP:

A) Police officers get angry, therefore, increasing negative tension and escalating behaviors. B) Arrest and jail time for people who fail to SLIP. C) Police officers might resort to the use of deadly force and shoot people who fail to SLIP. When police officers shoot people, they shoot to kill.

The third essential time for exposing children to SLIP Away from Harm principles is half way through high school-- preferably, the second semester of tenth grade. Tenth graders are usually 16-year-olds, and therefore, mature enough to handle real talk about staying out of trouble, and more importantly, life and death. 16-Years-old is a good time to implement SLIP Phase 3 principles because it is the appropriate age to introduce the fear factor into the equation of maintaining harmony with the police.

Of course, every child is different, so teaching styles depend on the child that you are dealing with, though. Nevertheless, under all circumstances, SLIP Phase 3 is the time to introduce reality based, self-preservation factors into SLIP Away from Harm lessons. Because SLIP Phase 3 targets high-schoolers, teach by using direct language which attempts to alter attitudes and behaviors--see SLIP Reference Chart 3 below.

Reference Chart 3.

SLIP Phase 3 Strategy:

Step 1) Here in this first step of the third phase of SLIP, keep it real and say to SLIP learners, "Always be nice and respectful to the police. Stay calm and cooperate each time you deal with the police because police officers are only human: sometimes they might be having a bad day, or maybe they are stressed-out. Whatever the reason is, if you sense that a police officer doesn't have proper patience, you must go out of your way and be extra patient and kind to the police officer. Your kindness will enable you to SLIP Away from Harm every time."

Step 2) Remember in SLIP Phase 2, Step 2, we emphasized, the police do not know who you are or what you think when they meet you. They can only judge you based upon how you act and follow instructions, so you must always act right and do what police officers tell you to do. When SLIP Phase 3, Step 2, is taught at age 16, revisit and reteach that same lesson of SLIP Phase 2, Step 2. Revisiting the information refreshes those SLIP concepts in the youngster's mind--no need to change a thing.

Step 3) SLIP Phase 3, Step 3, is the last SLIP awareness lesson for many school age children. Therefore, teachers must make it the most memorable lesson yet. Make a lasting impression on school age youngsters by instilling within their minds the following lifesaving information: "Police officers have very important jobs to do, so always stay calm and listen to them when they speak." Whether teaching SLIP Phase 3, Step 3 in a school setting or not, use this final opportunity to drive home the crucial messages while the students are yet

school age. A primary message is, "No matter how big or

strong we are, the police have us outnumbered, and the police

have many guns that they are trained to kill people with." The

ultimate message the student should take away from SLIP

Phase 3 is, "the police will shoot and kill people who do not

listen to, and cooperate with their instructions."

Now, here is a message to SLIP teachers. Do not shy

away from the elephant in the room. Make sure high schoolers

grasp this final takeaway from SLIP awareness lessons

because life and death depend on it. The following are the

cause and effect triggers of whether police officers shoot and

kill people, or not:

1) Police officers do not know you when they approach

you. They do not know what you are thinking or what you might

try to do. Therefore, always keep your hands empty and keep

your hands where police officers can see them at all times.

Police officers shoot and kill many people then report that they

thought the object in the victim's hand was a weapon.

2) Police officers can only judge you by the way you act. Therefore, stay calm, polite, and act sober.

3) The number one reason situations escalate is, people, fail to follow instructions of the police. When situations escalate, police officers draw their guns and shoot people. When police officers shoot people, they shoot to kill because mortally wounding people creates a final resolution, rather than injuring people. Police officers know, if they injure people, such people are likely to seek revenge via the court or other means. Like it or not, there is something to be said about the old cliché', "Dead men tell no tales." I know that all sounds a bit shady. Never mind the ethics, just be a good boy and don't get yourself shot. At the end of the day, the morgue is too cold, and hell is too hot, so just stay alive, and go home and hug your mother and your wife again--that is what they want you to do.

SLIP Phase 4 Strategy:

The fourth opportunity for exposing people to SLIP concepts is a premium, because of this time around, the learners should be mature and responsible enough to drive an automobile. SLIP Phase 4 Strategy should be emphasized to everyone upon the initial time they get a driver's license, and again when they renew their driver's license. Both parents and driver instructors should take advantage of the opportunity to emphasize the importance of SLIP concepts while they prepare new drivers for the challenges that lie ahead.

However, the best case scenario calls for DMV's involvement and influence. DMV is positioned to include SLIP information, tips, and references within driver study materials, each time drivers apply or reapply for a written driver's test.

Age relevancy is an important logistic for implementing SLIP. Adults, for the most part, are who they are already. Sometimes old, flawed ways of thinking and misguided stereotypes automatically doom people to stubborn behaviors that put them at odds with the police. Having said that, because so many killings by the police start out as a traffic related stop, why not make SLIP awareness one of the small prices to pay for receiving the privilege to drive.

Imagine the efficacy of advertisements sponsored by the Department of Motor Vehicles (DMV) or the National Highway Traffic Safety Administration (NHTSA) in writing and public video announcements which do not sugarcoat the reality of failing to SLIP. Why not feature SLIP ads which come right out and say things like: "Police officers have a very important job to do, therefore, always stay calm and listen to them when they speak? No matter how big or strong we are, the police have us outnumbered, and outgunned. The police have the power to shoot and kill people who do not listen to and cooperate with their instructions. We should always keep those thoughts in mind whenever we interact with the police."

If you think the preceding statements are a little rough around the edges, and not quite "PC" enough, take a few minutes and browse www.photographyisnotacrime.com and search, key word, killed by police. I dare you to watch one of those disturbing videos and observe the caveman mentality as it takes place. What you will see is clearly an "us, against them" saga that happens every day between citizens and the police. Consequently, you will begin to understand that the concept of something as simple as SLIP Away from Harm equates to an ingenious alternative.

4 Why Try SLIP

"If it is possible, as much as it depends on you, live peaceably with all men. Beloved, do not avenge yourselves, but rather give place to wrath: for it is written, 'Vengeance is Mine. I will repay,' says the Lord." Romans 12: 18-19.

We can all save lives going forward if we simply harness our God given power of compassion that dwells within us. The SLIP techniques which are taught in this book reminds us how easy we can make a difference by thwarting specific tragic incidents that dominate the national spotlight on a semi routine bases. The tragic incidents I'm talking about are the senseless, lose-lose epidemic of police officers and citizens killing each other.

Chapter three, covered at length how we should use SLIP techniques to systematically teach people how to survive. However, in the real world, you might have to seize whatever opportunity God gives you to try to save a life via SLIP teachings. That means, if you are a parent or guardian, sincerely teach your children to practice SLIP techniques during their early years. If you are a teacher or counselor, teach your pupils to SLIP. If you are a friend or mentor, tell your friends and acquaintances to SLIP.

The point is, recognize that you can bring about positive changes if you use whatever platform God gives you by seizing opportunities to teach SLIP techniques. Please remember this significant, final note: maximize your opportunities to use the church as a platform to teach SLIP techniques. The church offers many opportunities to raise awareness about SLIP, for instance: bible study classes, choir rehearsals, and last but not least, youth ministries. Empower the members within all of those individual ministries of the church to spread the word about SLIP to people who need the knowledge most.

The important thing to remember is, now is the time, start speaking up. Who knows, speaking up about trying to mend fences between broken police and community relations might save a life. Except for one or two high profile political figures, we live in a time when people are tentative and more sensitive about speaking up. Therefore, I will quantify what I am about to say with the following statement: I am a black man with a B.S. in Criminal Justice Administration and an M.A. in Human Behavior. Though, only briefly, I worked in law enforcement, before resigning while in good standing to pursue my college education and to do other things. Trust me; I speak with the voice of experience when I say, law enforcement work is not for everyone.

I have successfully raised a daughter, who now has a Ph.D., I thank God for that. Kudos to my daughter for working so hard. Presently, my wife and I are raising our 9-year-old son. My big, new idea for significantly reducing America's police deadly force problem is what I always have, and always will, teach my children: SLIP Away from Harm.

At the risk of sounding like, Captain Obvious, here: someone has got to have the intestinal fortitude to stand up and address the elephant in the room. Maybe it should be me, yet I wrestle with the notion of calling this elephant an elephant, just like everybody else wrestles with it. Sometimes it is politically incorrect to call things what they are, but here goes. In plain language SLIP means, whenever you deal with police officers: "Stop what you are doing, shut your mouth, open your ears and alert your brain. Do what police officers tell you to do--and you will live 99.9% of the times." That my friend is the elephant in the room.

Too many times these days, the elephant in the room goes ignored, and people are dying because of it. Before we can fix the elephant in the room, we as a community, and as a nation, have got to have the intestinal fortitude to say, "Hey, that elephant doesn't belong in this room. Why Is it here? Let's get rid of it, ASAP." Without a doubt, SLIP is the best way I know, methodically to get the elephant out of the room.

I am 100% certain; SLIP works, because I am a living testimony--many times over--and so is my daughter, who is the doctor in the family. In fact, I am already starting, subtly to teach SLIP awareness to my 8-year-old son, and I will always do the same for any friends that he hangs around. Who knows, the life that I save, might be my son's--and how great is that?

I wrote this new book about police with a newfound sense of urgency. Unlike in 2000, when I wrote my first book on police mistrust, this time around, I am focusing my efforts on creating positive attitudes via offering real solutions. One thing for sure, it is going to take real solutions to improve race relations between the police and communities. Most of all, though, I am laying out a plan in this book, which can reduce the number of loss human lives. After giving much thought to a mountain of facts and data, I have arrived at a four step system that can usher in significant improvements, going forward:

#1) I am most excited because, I am creating a new program that is extremely simple, which teaches grade schoolers how to: listen to and cooperate with, police officers. Thereby, avoiding harm to themselves, law enforcement, property, and others. Surprisingly, there is a void for such a program today, go figure. I'm super excited about filling the void of teaching children, on all three levels of grade school: elementary, middle school, and high school, how to be smart when confronted by police officers. The key is, make the program fun, interactive, and cool. I am certain, such a program will save lives in the long run, plus, it will improve police and community relations.

There is no time like the present, for creating a future generation who will be respectful to the police, at all times. By ingraining the principles of police trust and cooperation in our children, we create a subliminal, automatic default switch in their brains for dealing with situations that might happen down the road. We have the power to look into the eyes of the child that stands before us today, and impact his life in such a way, that it will save his life tomorrow. How can anyone who is a parent, not be excited about that?

Do you remember the D.A.R.E. Program? DARE stands for Drug Abuse Resistance Education. DARE was the leading children's social awareness program from 1983-2009. D.A.R.E.

was replaced with, keepin' it REAL (R.E.A.L.), in 2009. REAL, stands for Refuse, Explain, Avoid, and Leave. Just like those two programs, the system I propose is one that can be summed up as an acronym that makes for easy recollection.

In 2018, the next step in social awareness, teaching of children is long overdue because social programs have to evolve to keep up with the times. As I write this book about police and community relations, I am meticulously hammering out, what is, hopefully, the next big acronym and catchphrase: SLIP and SLIP Away from Harm. As stated before, SLIP stands for Stop and Listen to Instructions of the Police.

I'm happy to note, though, unlike DARE and REAL; SLIP requires no tax dollars because it is designed to be parent driven. Although school and police involvement are helpful and highly recommended, SLIP is designed to stand on its own. Parents and guardians simply get the book (and optional T-shirt, hat, or toy). Then, parents and guardians teach SLIP concepts to children and tell their friends using social media and word of mouth.

How essential are the concepts of SLIP? This big! The concepts might have eliminated every high profile case of police involved deaths that have sparked protests, like the NYPD's killing of 43-years-old, Eric Garner. Mr Garner's crime was selling cigarettes illegally/circumventing tax laws.

As reported by https://mobile.nytimes.com/2016/10/25/nyregion/justice-dept-replaces-investigators-on-eric-garner-case.html Mr Garner's death on July 17, 2014, marked the start of a succession of police killings that remain the focal point of national attention and debates over race and the police. For me to sit here and assign 100% of the blame for Mr Garner's death on Mr Garner would be unfair and irresponsible. However, who can argue that if he had followed the SLIP Away from Harm concepts, Mr Garner and his family would have had a lifesaving outcome of that situation? Just for a moment, let yourself imagine the avoidance of all the pain, suffering, and property damages if Mr Garner had the presence of mind to Stop, Listen to Instructions of the Police, on July 17, 2014.

Everything, mentioned in the preceding paragraph applies to April 12, 2015, when Freddie Gray, 25-years-old, died of spinal injuries that he suffered while in custody of Baltimore Police. Mr Gray's spine was 80% severed at his neck. Likewise, SLIP could have been a lifeline in the following cases: Michael Brown in Ferguson, MO., Walter Scott in North Charleston, S.C., Amadou Diallo in New York, and NFL linebacker Demetrius Dubose, who died by San Diego PD, etc. SLIP Away from Harm, held the key to the thwarting of each of those life ending tragedies.

#2) When deadly force is necessary, there must be no push-back from society. Such misguided push-back against the police for properly doing police work sends the wrong message to all people: good, bad, and indifferent.

#3) When it comes to deadly force, there is a need for greater public awareness: The problem of police brutality is not a racial issue, it is a serious crime called, excessive use of force. Excessive force has the potential to touch us all, one way or another, and sooner or later. For instance, none of us is immune to potentially having excessive deadly force take the lives of our mentally ill loved ones.

#4) Police officer training must undergo an evolution, starting at the top ranks, down to the bottom ranks. The wild, wild west simply doesn't meet the acceptable standard any longer. Taking human life has to be the last option on the table, every time. Let us begin to call excessive force precisely what it is: a crime. Punishment for excessive use of force by police officers must be firm, certain, and swift. Police officers who feel that not being able to use excessive force is a pill, too bitter to swallow, can quit because everybody wins when they quit.

After all is said and done, the bottom line is this: Here in the good old USA, we all should care about the police killing people because each year, more than 1,000 people are killed by the police. That means, there are thousands of babies, children, and teens, plus young and older adults who are destined to meet a horrific fate, of which we might be able to prevent if we develop an effective strategy. We all have the power, and therefore a duty to save lives. We must tell people, especially young men, to SLIP Away from Harm every time they deal with the police.

There is a much needed domino effect which comes with creating a population of citizens who choose to SLIP Away from Harm. When people do their part and cooperate with police officers, police officers walk away looking like good public servants, instead of villains. Hopefully, this will reduce violence against police officers and ease public tension. Our police system works best when our citizens and police officers, both, choose to keep things simple and respect one another. It is easier to subscribe to Matthew 5:38, "Eye for eye, and a tooth for a tooth," if you take that text out of context. The truth is, Matthew 5:38 must work in unison with Matthew 5:39 through 5:42, but you won't hear anybody bragging about, "I am going to follow the whole list of teachings from Matthew 5:38 - 5:42." And since it is not my place to preach a sermon, I urge readers of *SLIP* to read those bible verses and judge for themselves.

5 Deadly Force vs. Defiance

Whenever high strong people arm themselves to the teeth, packing lethal force as police officers, confront people who do not respond well to authority, expect the worst possible outcome. Why are we surprised, when police officers armed with lethal force butt heads with defiant individuals, the end result often is death? We can take that equation, one step further, and say, sometimes unwise men automatically default to defiance because they perceive that a police officer who singles them out, is a bully. Defiant behavior gets interpreted by police officers as disrespect, and once that happens, all bets are off because a caveman mentality takes over. Citizens should head these simple words of wisdom, "Agree with your adversary quickly, while you are on the way with him, lest your adversary delivers you to the judge, the judge hand you over to the officer, and you be thrown into prison." Matthew 5: 25

Police officers who get highly agitated by disrespect are subject to knee jerk reactions. Therefore, their natural reactions go something like this: "I'll show you, you annoying SOB." Then, out comes the gun and down goes the resister. The result is death. In impacted communities, though, many open-minded people feel, on a subliminal level, the last equation is easier to accept when a resister is a black person. These behaviors are ironic and difficult to understand because many of the police officers have black friends on the force, from former sports teams, or with whom they served in the military. That is why, knowing what goes on in the head of each police officer who uses excessive deadly force, is better examined on a case by case basis.

Here is another elephant in the room alert: It is dumb and dangerous to think that God cut all police officers from the same fabric. Police officers are creatures of the cultures perpetuated by upper management within their specific branches. Society has a duty to approach every case, wherein the appearance of the use of obsessive force might have occurred, with an open mind. Individuals in all types of professions, sometimes fail to do the right thing 24/7, why can't we allow ourselves to be open to that possibility when it is relevant to police officers?

Once again, it takes less than three minutes of your time to visit, the Killed by Police database at http://**killedbypolice.net**, therein, you will be amazed to see how many people, including their race and gender, who died at the hands of police. This website is especially enlightening because it also gives us the race and gender of the fallen.

I had to stop and ask myself, what is going on here? Are the police killing so many people because we are such bad human beings and deserve to be slaughtered or are a few police officers, such bad people, that they are committing murder because they know they can get away with it? That is a question that is worthy of exploration. Let's face it; the facts are what they are: according to **thinkprogress.org**, in 2015, the police killed approximately 1,200 people.

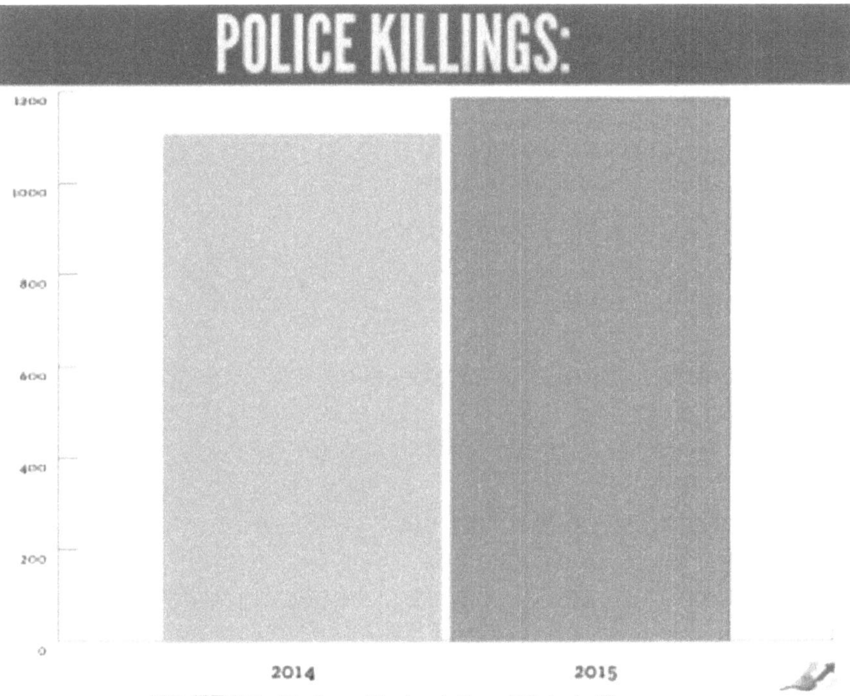

CREDIT: Dylan Petrohilos/Think Progress

You want to guess how many of the officers who took that many human lives got convicted of murder or manslaughter? If you guessed zero, you guessed correctly. Now, what do those facts tell us about law enforcement who took those lives? The facts tell us that all of those shootings were justified. But wait a minute, now.

Think back on the many disturbing videos we saw in the recent 36 months. Should we believe our eyes or not? If we believe our eyes, and we should, some of the cases had the appearance of excessive force, such as 25-year-old-Freddie Gray who died from spinal injuries suffered in police custody. Likewise, 32-year-old Philando Castile. The police stopped Mr Castile for a missing tail light--his girlfriend streamed the bloody aftermath video on Facebook. How about the video of 43-year-old, Eric Garner of the infamous NYPD choke hold. He was illegally selling cigarettes. And who can forget 40-years-old Terence Crutcher, the Tulsa, OK man who was fatally shot by a police officer even though, he was unarmed with his back facing the police officer and his hands were raised above his head as ordered when Officer Betty Shelby? Though the case looked like a slam dunk murder case back around September 16, 2016, seven months later Officer Shelby was found not guilty of manslaughter. And remember, manslaughter is a less hard to prove murder charge which carries a lesser sentence.

The preceding list of the disturbing videos is enough to open minds about possible questionable integrity in all professions. But if not, go to photographyisnotacrime.com key words: police officer plants evidence after the shooting or http://photographyisnotacrime.com/2015/04/07/south-carolina-cop-arrested-for-murder-after-video-shows-him-shooting-man-in-back/.

South Carolina Cop Arrested for Murder after Video Shows

Shooting Man in Back

You will see many issues of bad police officers planting evidence after killing people like North Charleston, S.C. Police Department's Michael Slager appeared to be doing after killing Walter Scott via shooting him five times in his back. Still, police officer Michael Slager's first trial ended in a mistrial because 11 jurors voted to convict him, but one juror refused to vote for conviction. In the weeks that followed, however, Michael Slager changed his plea to guilty of felony violating the civil rights of

Walter Scott. Michael Slager did so in federal court on May 2, 2017, as part of a plea deal that led to the dropping of two other federal charges that he faced, including murder.

As I alluded to before, back in the year, 2000, I wrote a book stating that police mistrust in specific communities is a big societal problem facing our great country. However, back then, little did I know, to what extent I was foreshadowing the near future? Obviously, my theme of that book, nearly 20 years earlier, was prophetic. Oh man, do we ever live with the consequence of those problems today, of which, I spoke so candidly about, back during those times? The book I wrote was about, what was then, too little talked about and too easily dismissed as sour grapes, and whining, whenever victims spoke out about it. I'm talking about police mistrust. In hindsight, I can see that police mistrust was the elephant in the room that no one wanted to acknowledge; however, due to cell phone cameras, police mistrust is widely known and ferociously debated today.

Back in 2000, when I published that book, on the one hand, I was bombarded with criticism for being too biased against law enforcement. On the other hand, people showered

me with praise for telling the truth about how things were. And

of course, often I was also met, somewhere in the middle, with

lukewarm acceptance, usually accompanied by words like,

"yeah, but," while people offered their critiques for better ways

to go about writing such hotly contested books. You know what,

though, all three of the before mentioned receptions of my little

book were right for offering their: criticism, praises, and

critiques. The point I'm painfully aware of today is, in the heat of

the moment, I underestimated the power of that opportunity to

generate the much needed element which was necessary to

extinguish the smoldering embers that were destined to go on

and become full fledge wildfires.

The extinguishing agent, I'm speaking of is none other

than, the power of dialogue. Oh man, I wish I was wise enough,

back in 2000, to realize that I had stumbled upon a dangerous

powder keg. That powder keg, which was ready to explode was

inadequate police conflict resolution. I failed to do my job, which

was, to continue to sound the alarm so that I could cause

people to acknowledge that trouble was lurking and we, as a

diverse nation, needed to talk about the situation, candidly. Who knows, maybe we could have avoided certain disasters which are too prevalent and commonplace today. Dare I say, probably many lives lost by police officers and the community could have been saved.

According to the pro-gun-control-Brady Campaign, as of May 2016, there was a 17% increase in fatal shootings of police officers. On the opposite side of the spectrum, 855 people were killed by the police as of 10/21/16--that is according to the Killed by Police database. FYI, approximately 1,200 people were killed by police in 2015, according to the Wall Street Journal.

What do these tragic problems have in common? Extensive and too often unruly protests which tend to spill over into rioting, and unsightly media coverage, which gives a black eye to North America's image around the world. For me, that is a list of avoidable problems that went unlearned, because I failed to push for more dialogue when I published my book on police mistrust, back in 2000. Imagine how much progress we can make toward fixing our police and community relations issues if we all try to participate in making the situation better.

Let's face it; America prides itself on pointing out to certain other nations; they should do a better job of handling human rights issues. Other nations are quick to hold a mirror up to America's face and say, "Take a look at yourself first, then come and talk to us after you have cleaned up your mess."

It is hard to believe, but 17 years have gone by since I wrote that little book about police mistrust, and now guess what? Mothers are still crying. And more so than ever. Believe me; this book is not my way of saying, "See; I told you so." I am mature enough to know; sometimes it is better to be wrong, rather than right. Oh, how much, I wish I were wrong? Unfortunately, though, I was right, because now, not only are we faced with broken families burying innocent citizens, but now, broken families are burying innocent police officers, as well. Wow, how prophetic was Rodney King, when he uttered those simple words: "Why can't we all, just get along?" That one-liner catchphrase immediately became the butt of many jokes, but now those words are not so funny anymore because people are often dying and they are dying too young.

By way of reflection, I am reminded that after separating honorably from the military, my first career job was in law enforcement. However, I often find myself saying, "What has happened to the truth and what is wrong with the truth?" The time has come when some basic analysis of the truth about police mistrust, must be explored. Common sense and good, decent ethics dictate that the truth must prevail for us to fix our police crisis in our great country.

If not now, then when, will the time come that a candid discussion about a new way of doing law enforcement work is necessary to answer the profound questions that video evidence crams into the brains of people on both sides of the police conflict resolution debate. After all of the posturing, spinning, denials, and outright lies about the true details of each tragic police shooting, video evidence, and truthful eyewitness testimony gives us enough facts to conclude the truth, almost every time. Unfortunately, though, like with politics in this country, one half of the country see one thing and the other half see the opposite.

Maybe a positive takeaway from all the madness of the violence against the police, and that perpetrated by the police, will be a seismic shift in our way of generalized thinking about the police. Face it; even rational people find it hard to get to the truth as long as the elephant in the room remains the dominant figure. In most instances, the elephant in the room that no one wants to talk about when it comes to the police is, there is an outright denial that law enforcement work is not for everyone who signs up for the job. The truth is, there are some individuals who are working as police officers who need to be dismissed from the ranks ASAP. All will benefit when police departments shed such ill equipped personnel from its ranks.

Getting back to the truth, what happened to civilized societies that retarded us from evolving beyond the point in which we feel compelled to cling to the absurd notion that we must have: all or nothing, black or white, my way or the highway. When it comes to deciding who is right and who is wrong, each time there is a police officer involved shooting, our brain's default becomes a one-way street. And that is so dumb. Obviously, there is a middle ground, and obviously, each case is unique, because we are talking about human behaviors.

To be fair, and to ruffle the least feathers, let's go on record and say, of course, a very high percentage of police officers are professional individuals who are sincere in their quest to protect and serve. Now, having said that who are we kidding when we make blanket statements which suggest that there are no specific individuals who end up working in law enforcement who are not suited for the job due to temperament, inferior conflict resolution skills, personal biases, etc.?

To be fair to both sides, sometimes I cringe when I see protesters on the news causing a big uproar regarding an officer involved shooting when obviously the person who got shot by the police, had it coming. I think to myself, don't the protesters know that they are doing a disservice to their cause by protesting the shooting of a person who was committing a dangerous criminal act? And in the kindest of words, let's suffice it to say, just let it go whenever a poor soul seals his fate via suicide by cop, or if a person otherwise provokes an officer

to shoot him as the last resort of the officer. Protestors have to

choose their battles selectively if their protests are to remain

meaningful. On the other hand, whenever it is obvious that a

particular shooting by a police officer of an unarmed person is

murder, no matter what the race or social status the victim is,

then protest is necessary.

By all means, give the devil his due when those poor

people in law enforcement have to use deadly force to save

themselves or to save the lives of others--that is the

unfortunate, but inevitable nature of police work. We should not

give police officers a hard time for doing their jobs, any more

than we would give firefighters for doing their jobs. One more

thing, there is something to be said about the cliché, "If you

don't like how the police are doing their jobs, and if you think

you can do it better, put down your protest signs and pick up a

law enforcement job application." If you don't know how to start

the process, it is as simple as, turning to the internet and going

online and answering some questions on a straightforward

application. Become a police officer yourself so that you can become a part of the solution. You have to admit, helping to fix our nation's ugliest social problem sounds like a good place to start, especially for those who feel extra passionate about such issues.

As for the truth, this is where the rubber meets the road. There's not enough honesty coming from local government officials and the media when bad police officers do bad things. A vast majority of the protests which take place in the aftermath of deadly police shootings, would not escalate, and indeed could be squashed all together, if more law enforcement agencies would join the latest trend and report a good heavy dose of transparency right up front. It starts by top law enforcement officials making statements like these: "The video footage is quite disturbing, and we will get to the bottom of this problem immediately. Rest assured, the details of this investigation will be as transparent and forthcoming as possible." In the end, what communities are looking for from ranking law enforcement officials is this statement: "We promise that justice will prevail in this matter."

It just looks scandalous and dehumanizing to the victimize communities when police officers, unites and speak using the voice of the police union; saying nothing went wrong here; this is just another case of a police officer doing his job. Such cold behavior is a dagger to peaceful solutions because the victimized community can see what's going on. People know a duck when they see one. Therefore, protests are the people's way of saying, "look at the evidence you fools: if it walks like a duck, quacks like a duck, and poops every five minutes; then obviously, it is a damn duck." The public is weary of seeing police unions give their blessings to an apparent murder of an unarmed victim on the day after the tragedy. Such actions by law enforcement deliver a kiss of death to peace and de-escalating of tensions involving the police.

The eyeball test goes a long way in determining whether a situation is going to become a disaster for the community as far as protests and riot concerns go. People are watching to see the quick, decent, and professional handling of sensitive situations—community officials should get it right, the first time. Let's face it, whether murder happens to the police or by the police; often it's not rocket science. Such times when murder is obvious, the public knows murder when they see it, so don't try to BS the public. Murder is still murder, no matter who does it, it is always a painful injustice that cuts like a knife for both citizens and the police. For instance, despite what Chicago Police Officer Jason Van Dyke would have us believe, he acted too hastily when he took the life of 17-year-old Laquan McDonald on October 20, 2014, via shooting him 16 times. Then the hot-headed officer conspired with other police officers to cover up the truth. So much so, it took 400 days to release the dashcam video to the public. No matter, though, Officer Van Dkye still faced six counts of first degree murder plus an indictment of 16 new criminal charges too. And oh, several of Van Dyke's coconspirators faced felony charges as well for their cover-up roles—too bad, because the conspiring officers did commendable police work on that case, outside of covering up the crimes of Officer Van Dyke.

Speaking of the eyeball test, on May 26, 2017, CBS This Morning aired a troubling video showing the tragic criminal Jailhouse treatment which led to the untimely death of 35-years-old Michael

Sabbie of Arkansas. Mr Sabbie was a father of four who died in the custody of the LaSalle Corrections bi-state jail on the Texas-Arkansas border back in July 2015. That video, which was given to CBS News by the victim's family attorney, was as obvious as could be in terms of cause and effect. Yet when mentioning the video, the press felt the need to preference it with this disclaimer, "this video is not yet validated," or similar words to that effect.

I found the disclaimer noteworthy because as clear as day, we saw a medically-vulnerable Mr Sabbie in medical distress. His distress was obvious because, during a 9-in-a-half minute video of the Jailhouse tragedy, Mr Sabbie complained 19 times (CBS News counted 23 times) that he could not breathe. Also, while crying for help 19 or 23 times, he repeatedly begged for water. If these egregious acts by the jail officials were not enough, Mr Sabbie was thrown to the floor by one guard and held down and peppers sprayed by six guards. Then he was rinsed off and taken to see the nurse for less than one minute.

Finally, the guards neglected to follow the mandated protocol of checking on Mr Sabbie via regular face-to-face 30-minute checks.

Likely, those standard 30-minute checks, if done responsibly, would have saved Mr Sabbie's life. In August 2016, the Department of Justice told the victim's widow that no charges would be filed in the case. Finally, in May 2017, the family filed a federal civil rights complaint.

One must admit, though, there don't seem to be any confusion around the eyeball test when police officers get shot down in the streets, like dogs. Rightfully so, each time tragedies happen to police officers, media reports give a detailed description of the shooter and say: "the suspect murdered a police officer," then the media goes on to say that "the police officer was married and leaves behind whatever number of children." That's a great reporting policy and that's the way it should be. On the other hand, it feels like law enforcement and the media look for words to vilify the victims when unarmed citizens are shot down by the police. Vilifying the victim killed by the police happens, no matter if the video is as clear as it can be. Statements about such victims always precede words like, "there will be an investigation to see what the outcome of the situation should be." People have reached a point now where they are very skeptical about the outcomes of such investigations. We are conditioned to expect an unfavorable outcome of investigations for victims who get shot or otherwise killed by the police. We know, more than nine times out of ten such investigation results are going to come back favorable to the police officers.

In concluding this chapter, let me clear up a few mysteries about the book that I wrote back in 2000. The book was called, "201 Reasons Not to Trust Police--The Crooked Ones." In a younger state of mind, I wrote that book in response to my growing anxiety due to the high profile police officer involved shootings, back then. However, the specific police officer shooting, which nudged me over the top with inspiration, so that I wrote: "201 Reasons Not to Trust Police--The Crooked Ones" was the fatal shooting of an ex-NFL football player who lived in San Diego back in 1999.The shooting victim's name was Demetrius DuBose. Two SDPD officers shot the young man 12 times, including five times in his back. Of course, officer reviews of those two shooting officers found the officers, innocent of all wrong doings in that case, as well.

6 **Policing the Mentally Ill**

I cannot in good conscience write this book in its entirety without talking about protecting the mentally ill via better policies and training within law enforcement. Now, more than ever, the need is so great for the public to push for the allocation of greater awareness, better police officer training, and resources for teaching the mentally ill how to SLIP Away from Harm. High performing, mentally ill people are fully capable of and are in need of empowerment of SLIP Away from Harm teachings.

The most relevant and timely source of information for this chapter's subject matter can be obtained by simply googling autismspeaks.org and searching the key words: law enforcement awareness. There, you will find all things; politically expedient, educational and awareness tools, technological breakthroughs, fund raising opportunities, localized and national programs. Here is a small sample of programs included: ALEC, 2015 Obama Task Force, Autism Awareness 9-1-1 First Responders Training, etc. As a reader of SLIP, you are a conscientious person. Therefore, I urge you to take a look at some the useful programs that are making a difference, and tell your friends.

In 2015, the Virginia-based, Treatment Advocacy Center released an alarming study, which reported that the police are 16 times more likely to kill people with mental illness compared to others. In other words, a mentally ill person is killed in about one of every four fatal police officer encounters. And according to the National Alliance on Mental Illness, 15% of men and 30% of women booked in U.S. Jails annually, suffer from mental illness. Thanks to *USA Today News* for those helpful statistics because many analytically minded people feel, the numbers speak louder than words. No matter who you are, I encourage you to keep those troubling statistics in mind as you consider such cases that are featured in *SLIP*. Also, keep those stats in mind as you contemplate the horrifying fears that face the family members of those living with mental illness, both now and going forward

Let's use the LAPD as a case study; based on a *Los Angeles Times* report, approximately 15,000 of the people LAPD arrested in 2013 were homeless. It is well documented through study after study, homelessness and mental illness share a symbiotic relationship. The 15,000 arrested by the LAPD equaled 14% of the total arrests made that year. Administrative office reports estimated the labor costs for making those arrests were estimated between $46 million and $80 million.

On top of that, Loss Angeles spends another six million dollars on the LAPD Mental Evaluation Unit. This unit consists of a team of mental health professionals and police officers who are supposed to intervene with the mentally ill and connect them to needed services. Here is the catch, though, these funds all come from an annual $100 million budget to combat homelessness by the city of Los Angeles. Like too many other cities that mean well, across the USA, Los Angeles is locked in a vicious cycle of feeding good tax dollars into a bottomless pit, every passing year. Such inefficient use of tax dollars is indicative of a clueless dog chasing its tail—round and round it goes, but in the end, it goes nowhere. The bottom line is we have far too many people with fancy titles who need to wake up and stop falling into the trap of trying to manage homelessness rather than finding solutions to end homelessness.

When it comes to mental illness and law enforcement issues, not only the homeless are at risk, though. For instance, let's take the fatal shooting case of Daniel Shaver. Although, his case is not about mental illness, Daniel Shaver's shooting by a Mesa, AR Police Officer is enough to send shockwaves across the lives of everybody who have mentally disabled loved ones. In order to understand what I mean by that statement, take a couple of minutes and view a video of that tragedy on the internet, then read a professional commentary on the case by James A. Gagliano. He is a retired FBI supervisory special agent and a CNN law enforcement analyst in addition to serving as an adjunct assistant professor at St. John's University in Queens, New York. The case is simple enough to find on the internet. Just Google the words: Daniel Shaver killed by police, commentary by James A. Gagliano.

Witness first hand and observe a young man's final seconds of life as he pleads for mercy, but he finds none. So afraid for his life, was the young man—sounds like he was fighting back tears—as he tried desperately to convince the would-be shooter through humble agonizing verbal cues like, "You're going to shoot me!" Then see for yourself, one hyper emotionally charged police officer responds, "Shut up! I'm not here to be tactful or diplomatic with you. You listen. You obey." Then the officer aims his loaded gun and squeezes the trigger, striking Daniel Shaver five times. It was as though the shooter was just a hunter who was taking the life of big game prey in the wilderness. The million dollar question is, if this was a mentally ill person, how in the hell could he or she survive this encounter? That is one of the most bothersome aspects of this shooting, and there are so many others.

Go ahead, and watch for yourself, but be forewarned that you will have to ask yourself; am I really seeing what I'm looking at here? You'll likely say to yourself, I know that I didn't just watch an individual—so high on the power of his position—take the life of a very frightened, unarmed human being—while the human being was crying out for mercy. If you are humane, you will wonder; "What kind of healthy, rational thinking, law-abiding man could do that to another good man?" Here is a hint into the clueless mindset of such a person. He is the man who has the words "You're F*****" engraved on the barrel of his personal, department-approved AR-15.

I guarantee you, you will be fascinated by the background of the shooting police officer. You'll be dumbfounded by the dangerous and idiotic loopholes in the justice system. And you will be confused by the legally sanctioned, savage-like actions and attitude towards ending human life based purely on one's job title. Last but not least, you will see that civilized norms and common decency mandates that standardized, better training is desperately needed nationwide.

The city of El Cajon is a suburb of San Diego, CA. On September 27, 2016, the El Cajon Police Department (ECPD) shot and killed an unarmed mentally ill man, name Alfred Olango, a 38-year-old father of two. The fact that Mr Olango was an unarmed black man was the theme that resonated most. However, there were two different variables regarding that case which concerned me most. First, Mr Olango was unarmed and second; he was mentally ill. The date ECPD, killed Mr Olango; he was suffering a mental breakdown, to the extent; it prompted his sister to call 911 for assistance. His sister was careful to articulate with great emphasis that her brother, Mr Olango, was suffering mental duress.

Such mental illness crises and situations, mandate that ECPD should dispatch qualified PERT personnel. Instead, they sent two officers to deal with the situation who were ill equipped to handle the circumstances. PERT, stands for Psychiatric Emergency Response Team. Ironically, a grand jury had recommended improvements in ECPD's treatment of the homeless and mentally ill approximately one year before its officers shot and killed, Mr Olango. Clearly, there is a pressing need for directing more resources and attention to creating and

expanding Crisis Intervention Teams (CIT) throughout law

enforcement in general. In addition, wider use of less lethal

police tools like Electric Control Devices (ECD, such as tasers)

and training police officers to exercise tactical retreat (stepping

back and containing a situation) are options that must be

attempted prior to resorting to deadly force.

An attorney for Mr Olango's family reported that ECPD

selected a single still-shot photo from video footage and used it

as a tool to muddy the waters by tainting public opinions

towards Mr Olango's guilt. That photo, as seen across the

nation via the internet and other news platforms, shows Mr

Olango standing in a shooting position pointing an e-cigarette

at an ECPD Officer. Common logic leads one to say, well then,

there you go--that's why the police officer shot and killed that

man. However, the problem with that theory is, the police

officers were notified that they were responding to a mental

illness breakdown crisis. Therefore, despite the fact that ECPD

would have us believe, Mr Olango's final actions resulted in him getting tased by one officer and fatally shot five times by the second officer, the victim should have been confronted by PERT personnel.

The truth is, there were a plethora of mistakes made by both the victim and the police. As such, there is blame to go around as well. However, our society must assign the weight of the blame in this particular case to ECPD because, at the end of the day, ECPD took the life of a human being, when clearly other options should have been on the table. We must require more of our police departments because we can do better. In everyday layman's language, we cannot have police officers going around shooting crazy people just because they are crazy--we are not living in Hitler's Nazi Germany.

The list of mentally ill victims killed by the police is both long and disturbing. Another high profile case which comes to mind is that of a 43-year-old father of seven, Keith Scott, killed September 20, 2016, by an officer of Charlotte-Mecklenburg Police Department (CMPD). Mr Scott reportedly suffered mental impairment caused by a traumatic head injury due to wrecking his motorcycle into a tree in November 2015. Officer

Brentley Vinson, was the police officer who shot and killed Mr Scott. For the sake of racial understanding, in this case, the police officer was black, and the victim was black, as well.

I chose to single out this particular case because it has all of the main ingredients of your typical run of the mill "police shoots black man" cases. However, once you examine the details more closely, this case takes on many layers of complexities that are unique and alarming. Number one, yes a police officer took the life of a black man, again. But a closer look at this case reveals a black cop was the killer. Number two, it was said that the black man had a firearm in his possession at the time he was shot and killed by the police. However, contrary to police statements, eyewitness testimony, records that the victim was not brandishing a firearm when he was shot and killed by the police.

Number three, police officer statements claim that the black man failed to cooperate with the police. A closer look at this case reveals that the black man suffered from mental impairment due to head trauma. Compassionate thinkers are left wondering, how much impact Mr Scott's documented mental illness played a role in his behavior during those final minutes of his life. It would be nice to know how mental diminishment affected the variables of cause and effect that day so that we could use that knowledge gained, to help other sick people and improve police department PERT training, going forward.

Summing up Mr Scott's case, once again, at the end of the day, no charges were brought against a police officer who shot and killed a human being. An article in https://www.nytimes.com/2016/11/30/us/charlotte-officer-acted-lawfully-in-fatal-shooting-of-keith-scott.html, Susanna Birdsong, the policy counsel for the ACLU of North Carolina, said the decision not to bring charges demonstrates the need for policies to ensure that officers "employ de-escalation tactics, avoid implicit bias and take into account how mental disabilities can affect a person's behavior."

The primary parting shots in this chapter and this book are: 1) Alternative policing like PERT and CIT, tactical retreat and ECD deserve all the publicity, education, and resources possible from us as citizens and the media. 2) The biggest question about modern day policing and mental illness is: are we doing enough to prepare for what likely lies ahead regarding the growing epidemic of people living with Autism Spectrum Disorders (ASD)?

Since alternative policing methods have been covered already, the remainder of *SLIP* is dedicated to shedding light on ASD and the criminal justice system. The information that is forthcoming provides a foundation that is eye opening for readers who are fortunate enough to have no clue about ASD because it has not touched them yet. The information is both reinforcing and enlightening for people who have extensive knowledge of ASD. As for those readers whose knowledge of ASD falls somewhere in between those two extremes, the information is an essential educational tool.

The information that I am going to share with you, is the expert advice from someone who is far greater qualified to speak on the lofty subject of ASD and the criminal justice system than I am. The source of the information is in the form of a professional article that readers can easily access via google, and I strongly encourage readers to do so. The creator of the article is Barbara J. Doyle, Master of Science Degree. I have written the gist of the article, but I hope that readers will locate the original article and read it in its entirety. To locate the article, simply go to autismspeaks.org and search for the article by title, or google the article by title, *And Justice for All: Unless You Have Autism.* This article helped me tremendously and I believe there is some useful information in it that can benefit all.

The complete title of the article is *And Justice for All: Unless You Have Autism--What the Legal System Needs to Know about People with Autism Spectrum Disorders.*

Points to Remember:

"The diagnosis of an autism spectrum disorder (autism, autism spectrum disorder, pervasive developmental disorders, Asperger Syndrome and related disorders) is ALWAYS relevant and needs to be explained to police and legal personnel.

If an individual has been assessed to be "autistic like" or to have "autistic tendencies," providers and families need to explain the features of ASD that the person does have. It is safest to do the same type of explaining as you would if the person carried an official diagnosis of an ASD.

A diagnosis of an ASD is as relevant to police and legal proceedings as a diagnosis of mental retardation or mental illness would be, no matter how bright, high functioning, and/or verbal the individual may be.

A diagnosis of an ASD means that the person does have a developmental disability if the criteria for developmental disability are met, even if there is no mental retardation.

A diagnosis of an ASD is very important no matter what other diagnosis the individual carries.

If a person with an ASD is involved in legal or police matters, others who know the individual well needs to quickly provide information about how the individual thinks, communicates, interacts and understands others. Always provide that Information in writing AND in person to all authorities involved.

Each person with an ASD is unique. However, they share some common features. Assess to determine the impact of autism on the individual.

The individual will usually be responding to the best of her or his neurological ability at that time and in that place. Types of responses to others may not be optional, but more driven by internal state, sensory input, and previous learning.

People with an ASD respond and perform neurologically inconsistently depending on the emotional state, familiarity with the people and situations and various sensory experiences. For example, they may be very talkative in one setting at a particular time and later be UNABLE to speak well in the same setting."

Legally Relevant Features of ASD Diagnoses:

(Readers will see potential problem behaviors here, but readers can see the actual article for results of behaviors)

1. People with a diagnosis on the autism spectrum have significant problems is both verbal and non-verbal communication and in both sending and understanding

messages. This results in behavior that needs to be explained and understood as such:

The individual's facial expressions and body language will not necessarily reflect the internal state or emotions of the individual. The effect may be flat or "fixed" into a grin or grimace.

The individual with ASD may not respond in a typical way to the facial expressions, gestures, the tone of voice, or physical proximity of others.

The individual may interpret what is said in, literally, missing information that is inferred or implied.

The individual may have problems understanding the passage of time and in being able to distinguish between what is known NOW and what was known at some time in the past.

The individual may use out of context speech, talking about a topic that seems tangential or irrelevant.

The individual may have memorized whole segments of language and movements from movies and television. The individual may use this memorized speech at inappropriate times when something from the present reminds him of the scene in the movie.

The individual may have greater expressive language skills than receptive language skills. This means s/he may be able to say more than s/he actually understands (or vice versa).

The individual may have formal or odd and pedantic speaking habits. If someone sneezes, for example, the individual may tell a judge or police officer that he should say "God Bless You" in a way not appropriate for the circumstances.

The individual may have memorized responses to certain communicative invitations (i.e. no matter the circumstances, ASD individuals might always say "I'm fine" whenever asked, how are you?).

The individual may take what others say to them "at face value" (i.e. ASD individuals might be easily tricked).

2. People with a diagnosis in the autism spectrum experience significant problems in social interaction and reciprocity. This results in behavior that needs to be explained and understood as such:

The individual may not answer immediately when spoken to or may not consistently respond to initiations of others.

The individual may not use eye contact in a typical way. S/he may prolong eye contact in what is to others an uncomfortable way or may avoid eye contact.

The individual may not respond to or use social conventions such as greetings, handshakes and topics, use for social "small talk."

The individual may not shift topic when the conversational partner does so leading others to assume that the individual is self-absorbed.

The individual may have problems distinguishing what is known NOW from what was known in the past. Once the individual with ASD knows what has happened, they may be unable to recall a previous time when they did not have that knowledge.

The individual may be unable to predict the behavior of others by looking at them or listening to them.

The individual may be guileless and easily led or shaped by others if the individual is led to believe that there will be a positive outcome.

3. People with a diagnosis on the autism spectrum will be likely to have restricted, repetitive, stereotypes and unusual patterns of interests, behavior and activity. This results in behavior that needs to be explained and understood as such:

The individual may not shift topic at the lead of another person or may keep coming back to the same topic many times in a repetitive way.

The individual with ASD may be "rule bound" and feel a strong need to obey learned rules.

The individual may Experience "sensory overload." This results from too much sensory input coming into the brain at one time. Sometime the brain of the person with ASD cannot cope with all of the input all at once. People with ASD describe this as becoming very overwhelmed quite suddenly and as a kind of "shut down." It may be similar to a panic attack. During sensory overload, the individual may not be able to take in more information or understand what is said. This situation can lead to extreme behavior such as running out of a room or trying to hit or push others away, unintentionally injuring self or other. The individual may over-react when touched by another person, particularly if the touch was unexpected, sudden or from behind.

The individual with ASD may have a "delay in processing" information that is told to them. This delay may result in not immediately responding to orders or commands and may lead others to assume that the individual is refusing to comply and unnecessary punishment or force may be used. The delay in processing usually increases in times of stress or in unfamiliar circumstances.

Case Scenarios:

Here are some case stories (with some features changed to protect privacy) that illustrate the need for police and legal system officials to have a full understanding of the impact of an autism spectrum disorder.

1. A young man with a diagnosis of pervasive developmental disorder lives in a small town. He likes a young woman in the town. He often goes up to her and talks about his

favorite topics (restricted interests). She tries to "brush him off" but he misses the subtle social cues (social interaction problem). He begins to wait for her in places where she is likely to be, just so he can see her (repetitive behavior). She feels stalked and harassed. She tells him she has a boyfriend but this does not deter his attentions (does not understand what is inferred). He feels happy when he sees her and thinks that maybe someday she will be his girlfriend like Superman was to Lois Lane (confusion with what was seen in movies, and innocence not in keeping with his other skills and age).

The young woman files a restraining order. This upsets the young man and he decides to write a note of apology and put it on her desk at the office where she works, while she is out to lunch (rule bound, he is "supposed" to apologize). He does so, violating the restraining order and is arrested. Later, when asked why he violated the restraining order he insisted that he did not. It had been explained to him that he had to stay away from "her." In his mind, he did stay away from her. He just went close to her desk (literal interpretation of language).

2. A young man with a diagnosis of high functioning autism (HFA) plays on a co-ed basketball team in his neighborhood. The other young men recognize how unworldly, he is and decides to play a trick on him (socially naive). They tell him that it is the birthday of a pretty, young woman on the team. They tell him that she loves birthday spankings, particularly on her bare bottom. They tell the young man with HFA that if he spanks the girl on her bare bottom she will probably kiss him and be his girlfriend.

After the game, the young man with HFA approaches the girl. He sings Happy Birthday to You (rule bound) while trying to pull down her shorts, and spanks her. The young woman screams and other people restrain the young man with HFA. He is terrified and becomes aggressive trying to defend himself from what he believes to be an unprovoked attack (sensory overload). Several people are injured. He is arrested for battery and sexual aggression.

3. A young woman with a diagnosis of Asperger Syndrome is in a small shop and sees a purse that she knew her mother wanted to have. She decides to take it to her

mother. She intended to pay the next year because she had seen a sign on the shop window that said, "Take home what you want today with no payments until January of next year!" (Confused by literal interpretation, language misunderstanding, and missed inference). She is arrested for shoplifting.

In court, she sits very still. She avoids eye contact with the judge and lawyers and only sometimes answers when spoken to (social reciprocity problems). Her face has a fixed grin type of expression on it (non-verbal communication issue) and she continuously lines up some pencils on the table appearing to be fully concentrated on this task (restricted, repetitive behavior). The judge gives her the maximum penalty possible stating that her grin was an insult to the court, that she did not pay attention to the proceedings and that she showed no remorse.

4. A woman described all of her life as "autistic like" has a car. She lends the car to a man who tells her that he wants to use it to go buy groceries for his family. The man commits serious crimes while using the car. Later, the woman is arrested as an accomplice. Her attorney decides not to mention

the "autistic like" diagnostic information to the court because he believes the court would think that the attorney was trying to prejudice the court.

In court, the woman displays a flat affect and shows no apparent response, no matter how serious or upsetting the testimony becomes (nonverbal communication problems). She does not speak when spoken to in court (inconsistent neurological functioning and issues in social reciprocity). When the judge asks her if she knew what the man planned to do when he borrowed her car, she answers "yes" (literal minded: he was going to buy groceries for his family, another possibility is that she NOW knew that he had committed the crimes and was unable to perceive a time when she did not have that knowledge). The judge remands her to a medium security prison for the maximum term as an accomplice. He cites her lack of concern and remorse and her knowledge before the fact of the crimes the man had intended to cost while using her car. Later, the man who committed the crimes is set free after a technical mistrial. However, the young woman with autism remained in jail.

Though, disastrous and troubling, the legal problems in the cases above did not present life and death challenges to the victims. Still, there is a great elephant in the room, just lurking in the shadows. The elephant is; what is going to happen when and if a substantial number of adults living with ASD find themselves face to face with the business end of a police officer's firearm? The latest data shows, children are being diagnosed with ASD at an alarming rate, one child in every 59. Exponentially, those numbers are increasing each passing year, for now. What does the future hold for these people when they become adults? I pray to God above; our policing system will not resort to doing, essentially what, the evil Adolf Hitler, did to disabled people. History shows, Hitler found it fitting to shoot and kill, disable people to eliminate them from society.

The case of a perfectly innocent, 14-year-old autistic boy getting roughed up by an undertrained police officer, who mistook him for a drug user, in Buckeye, AZ, provides a textbook case study for all to learn invaluable lessons. Geographically, Buckeye is a city of about 64,000 people, located in west Phoenix. The first lesson learned; an autistic teen was exhibiting very basic and easy to spot behaviors that are widely known by professionals and people who care about doing things the right way when responding to people who have mental disabilities. For instance, anybody who knows anything at all about autistic individuals should immediately think; "Let me rule out autism in this situation before I hastily jump to the wrong conclusion and do something inappropriate." The second lesson learned; there are a few basic people skills which are absolutely necessary for responding to individuals with mental disabilities because those skills provide the foundation that is needed for instantly recognizing relevant traits and tendencies. Such skills must be acquired through training and repetition drills. Those relevant skills provide the necessary platform for police officers and other first responders to instantly recognize what might be going on, in real time. Until and unless such relevant skills are learned and utilized, of course, police officers will continue the pattern of resorting to typical knee-jerk overreactions just like the Buckeye police officer did when he hastily jumped to the wrong conclusion. Let's not forget, though, in an odd but typical fashion, soon after the colossal blunder, the Buckeye Police Department, doubled down and went on to make bold statements proclaiming that the police officer did nothing wrong in this case.

A quick reality check of this disturbing case suggests, a police officer whose expertise is recognizing drug use, became so confused that he roughed up a sick boy just because he mistook him for a drug user suspect. That is a downright scary fact, but it is, nevertheless, the elephant in the room. Don't you think so? Rational, unbiased, and fair-minded people must take pause and think, "Oh my! Hey Captain, who the hell is minding the ship here? And, is this the best you've got? I sure hope not!" The boy's family got it right when they uttered the following statement to the press as they understandably demanded an apology and more police officer training: "This is as clear an example of inadequate training and supervision as you'll ever see." That was the heartfelt quote from the family of Connor Leibel in a statement to KPNX, an affiliate of NBC. I second that sentiment. And I'll add to those words by saying the following: such poor judgement demonstrates how inept current training methods are. The end result is; under current training practices, police officers lack the mental tools to demonstrate the necessary level of skills to observe and react in real-time situations when dealing with mentally disabled people. There is no surprise when operating under the cloak of ignorance, even good police officers find it difficult to navigate the murky waters of who is who, and what is what. Now throw in the fact that some police officers don't have the mental makeup to do the Job professionally in the first place — the end results translate to chaos, brutality, improper arrests, and wrongful deaths/murder. An unfortunate byproduct of all that madness is; law enforcement takes yet another black eye, both nationally and worldwide, under the shadows of widespread protests.

This case is uniquely relevant because so many families, in today's world, are impacted one way or another by mental illness, such as autism. This case causes such families to take pause and ask themselves: "Wow, what does the frightening outcome of this case mean for me and my family -- are we at risk of ending up on the painful end of a similar unfortunate mix up with law enforcement?" Also, who is asking the question: "What is it going to take to make law enforcement appreciate the need to better train front-line employees on the subject of dealing with disabled citizens, more seriously?" I hope it doesn't take a string of tragic events getting caught on video. No matter how organizations spin it, these complex problems can only be solved from the top down to the bottom.

In this case, the particular behavior that the 14-year-old autistic boy exhibited, which landed him in handcuffs, is simply called "Stimming." Stimming is short for self-stimulatory behavior and self-stimulation. Stimming manifests itself via repetition of physical movements, sounds, or repetitive movement of objects. This behavior is quite common in individuals with developmental disabilities, but most prevalent in people with autism spectrum disorders (ASD). The purpose of stimming is to cause a calming effect. Stimming is known in psychiatry as a "stereotypy." Any responsible training for police officers that involve dealing with people with developmental disabilities must consist of how to recognize stimming behaviors. Not only is stimming one of the DSM IV listed symptoms of autism, it is also observed in 10% of non-autistic children. The CDC puts the numbers at 1 in 59 school age children, over 1.3 million children under 18-years-old has ASD. You can imagine the astronomical number of folks who are older than 18-years-old who lives with ASD. Now add them to the mix and obviously that is a large number of people. We cannot have people walking around with loaded guns who must deal with these people, who don't even know what to look far or what they are dealing with -- that my friend, is a recipe for disaster. Despite claims made by the

Buckeye Police Department, that it trains its officers to recognize persons with disabilities, obviously, whatever training they are implementing needs to be reexamined and retooled.

If you missed the Connor Leibel story, here are the details of the case of the Buckeye, AZ police department and the autistic boy. The incident took place on July 19, 2017, because a police officer observed a teenager alone in a park "moving his hand to his face in a manner consistent with inhaling." The body cam video is easily locatable on the internet. Watching the video gives us an excellent milestone marker of how little the public and the police officers know about dealing with mentally disabled people. Likewise, watching the video shows us how great the distance is that we must travel before we arrive at a safe destination for treating people with disabilities with the kind dignity they deserve.

As you watch the video, remind yourself, that the officer who makes the mistake of using excessive force on this sick child -- and it was a mistake -- is a "so called" highly trained expert in recognizing people who are using drugs. However, I'm more inclined to agree with the professional opinion of the boy's family attorney who said in a letter, "I disagree with the department's finding that the officer did nothing wrong." Also, the attorney went on to say the officer in question, appears to have had literally no training in distinguishing between suspected drug users and citizens who suffer from developmental disabilities like autism."

You can see via the video that the boy was physically hurt badly by the unnecessary encounter with the police officer. As a professional human behaviorist, I can tell from the way the boy initially reacted to the police officer that the boy was totally frightened and confused. Furthermore, at 14-years-old, the boy likely had limited, but rigid impressions about the police. For instance, he probably had just enough knowledge about dealing with police officers to know that such an interaction can be very dangerous if police officers think you are doing something wrong. Of course, on the other hand, the boy probably also had been taught that interacting with police officers can be very helpful when you need help. Based on the way this boy reacted to the police officer -- backing away and repeating scripted words -- he felt he was in a dangerous situation with the police officer. The boy initially answered the police officer's question of: "What's going on?" to the best of his ability by saying, "I'm stimming." Then, once the police officer continued to move towards the boy and press him about his stimming behavior the boy became totally freaked-out and due to physical duress and suffering, he could only repeat, "I'm OK," over and over, and scream.

This is a really sad situation that only God knows how unnecessary or tragic it might have turned out if the boy's caregiver did not show up just when she did. The caregiver showed-up and let the clueless police officer know that the boy has autism. She told the police officer that the boy was stimming, then the officer told her, "I don't know what that is." Thank God, the caregiver was able to bring level-headed rational influence to the situation. Before she showed-up, this situation was completely void of level-headedness and rational judgement. Let's face it, we had an innocent mentally ill child getting roughed-up by an ignorant police officer who was convinced he was dealing with a drug addict/thug. You can see where this was heading; quick, fast, and in a hurry. The situation was headed toward a scenario wherein a police officer perceived he had a suspect who continued to not cooperate. Too often these situations don't end well. In this case the suspect didn't cooperate because he didn't know how to cooperate. And on the other hand, we had a police officer who would not allow himself to acknowledge he was not dealing with a druggy. This was due to the fact that his "precious drug use recognition training" was telling him he had caught a drug user abusing drugs, in the park in the daylight. Now you tell me; if that is not a recipe for disaster, what is?

A good take away from the Leibel case is; there is a meat and potatoes message for preventing the recurrence of such unfortunate pain and suffering that was caused in the Leibel case. That message is; police officers must receive proper training to recognize people who suffer from diseases like autism. Otherwise, police officers cannot know how difficult and sometimes impossible it is for people with disabilities to speak out loud the words they are thinking inside their heads. Another huge communication epiphany for police officers to realize is this; most likely -- and I mean nearly every time -- people with such disabilities need extra time (without any pressure at all) to answer "Wh" questions. Specific training is needed to educate police officers about certain common words that typical people take for granted which present communication stumbling blocks to people living with intellectual disabilities. "Wh" questions (what, where, who, which, and when) can present unique challenges to people with disabilities. In the video captured in this case, we can hear the police officer asking the boy, "What are you doing?" Obviously, there is no harm in asking anybody that question. However, police officers need to be trained to spot such uniquely odd behaviors like stimming because as we saw in this case, some good people might get hurt due to poor communication skills. Communication is the biggest challenge for many disabled people, but at the same time, it is essential for law enforcement and citizen interactions. A brief lesson, accompanied by a little follow-up refresher training goes a long way towards enabling police officers to know about simple communication strategies, such as a technique called OWLing (Observe, Wait, and Listen). Equally important is training police officers to stay away from the following behaviors: hasty conclusions, rushing, impatience, and heavy-handedness. Those negative behaviors will result in counterproductive results every time when dealing with people with developmental disabilities.

There is a need to end this story about the Leibel case in Buckeye, AZ on a positive note. First, we must remember that the problems, in this case, resulted from miscommunication. There was never a bad intention on the part of law enforcement. Second, I applaud the Buckeye police department for saying that the department officials are in the process of implementing "a voluntary registry of persons who suffer mental health crises in an effort to better respond and care for those in the community." That single statement tells me that they get it, never mind any other words or posturing exhibited by the Buckeye police department, they now know that they need to do a better job. In other words, a lesson learned. The registry is a smart way to go because it involves the community in a hands-on approach. The bottom line is; ensuring the safety of people who lack the capacity to think for themselves is a problem that takes both the community and law enforcement working together. Neither party can achieve maximum positive results in this crisis without the support and understanding from the other party. Finally, also happening in the great state of AZ is a program called "Be Safe." This program is run by Cynthia Macluskie, vice president of Autism Society of Greater Phoenix. This program is smart due to many reasons, but above all, it serves as a platform for bringing together families of those with autism and law enforcement. The program was formed in response to two Mesa, AZ police officers shooting and killing 24-year-old Danielle Jacobs, who suffered from

Asperger's syndrome. In addition, I strongly support Cynthia Macluskie's idea about people with ASD wearing an official bracelet that is easily identified because it increases their recognition to first responders

Last, but certainly not least, all are encouraged to connect with the National Center on Criminal Justice & Disability (NCCJD) (also called The Arc) and get involved. Getting involved is most likely unrealistic, on the other hand, all will certainly benefit from learning about the wide variety of resources that the NCCJD offers. Maybe the information and resources are not of use to you personally; however, chances are someone in your circle of family, friends, and colleagues have loved ones living with ASD or other disabilities.

No conversation about autism is complete without a discussion about the amazing contributions of Autism Speaks. Let me leave you with an article that comes to us via Autism Speaks (Family Services – Information for Law Enforcement). This article is comprised of the words of Dennis Debbaudt, Autism Risk & Safety Management. You can easily find this and other works by him on the internet, but I felt strongly enough about this article that I'm sharing (the gist of the article) it in "SLIP." The article is called "Information for Law Enforcement."

Police officers are usually the first to respond to an emergency. It is critical that they have a working knowledge of autism, and the wide variety of behaviors individuals with autism can exhibit in emergency situations. For instance, a person with autism might:

- Have an impaired sense of danger.

- Wander into the water, traffic, or other dangers.

- Be overwhelmed by police presence.

- Fear a person in uniform (ex. Fireman's gear) or exhibits curiosity and reach for objects/equipment (ex. Shiny badge or handcuffs).

- React with "fight" or "flight".

- Not respond to "stop" or other commands.

- Have delayed speech and language skills.

- Not respond to his/her name or verbal commands.

- Avoid eye contact.

- Engage in repetitive behavior (ex. rocking, stimming, hand flapping, and spinning).

- Have sensory perception issues.

- Have epilepsy or a seizure disorder.

Identifying that a person has autism is key for first responders because recognizing the characteristics helps them respond and offer proper support for the individuals.

For Law Enforcement

Tips for interacting with a person with autism:

- Be patient and give the person space.

- Use simple and concrete sentences.

- Give the person extra time to process and respond.

- Watch for signs of increased frustration and try to eliminate the source if possible to ensure that behaviors don't escalate.

- Avoid quick movements and loud noises.

- Do not touch the person unless absolutely necessary.

- Listen to caregiver, if available, to find out how to best respond.

Tips for general training guidelines:

- Law enforcement agencies should proactively train their sworn workforce, especially trainers, patrol supervisors, and school resource officers, to recognize the behavioral symptoms and characteristics of a child or adult who has autism, and learn basic response techniques.

- A training program should be designed to allow officers to better protect and serve the public and make the best use of valuable time, and avoid mistakes that can lead to lawsuits and negative media scrutiny, loss of confidence from the community, morale problems, and lifelong trauma for all involved.

-A good autism recognition and response workshop is designed to inform law enforcement professionals about the risks associated with autism, and offers suggestions and options about how to address those risks.

The most important thing citizens, particularly family members, who are concerned about the police treatment of those living with mental illness, can do, is be proactive. Families can be proactive by having a voice in alternative policing programs such as

PERT, CIT, and whatever programs exist for the sake of preventing lethal force by overly aggressive and under trained police officers. It doesn't take much effort to find out how much money your police departments in your surrounding area spend on alternative policing programs. Don't be afraid to think outside the box when you see alternative policing programs not receiving the funding they need. Families can go so far as to raise money for underfunded policing programs via GoFundMe campaigns and donations. Hopefully, the message is clear, families should call awareness to and put pressure on police departments to adequately fund and staff alternative policing programs by any means necessary.

Looking forward to our more civilized and humane society now is a perfect time to raise the question, what is law enforcement doing to prepare and respond to the unique intellectually disabled people who are destined to enter the adult world, seeing things and situations through a uniquely different perspective. Surely, under trained and under educated police officers coming in with guns blazing like the old wild, wild west; shooting first and asking questions later, will lead to disastrous outcomes.

7 A SWAT Officer's Advice

Have you ever stopped to think, why do some police officers act the way they act? If you haven't, and yet, you are a concerned citizen, you definitely should give some thought to why certain police officers overreact under certain circumstances. In my sincere attempt to walk a mile in the shoes of police officers, figuratively speaking, I dared to ask myself, why? You might want to ponder the question; why do certain police officers do the things they do? If for no other reason, just do it so that you might begin to understand the world as police officers see it. When you're up to the challenge, I recommend that you take a little time and do two things. The first thing, I'll say, is a must. So if you can only find the time or the energy to do one of the two things that I suggest here, I'll say you should read Black and

Blue, by SWAT Officer Tommy Holt, Jr. No doubt in my mind, this book will open your eyes to the complexities of police and community relations.

The second thing I'd recommend that you do is to accompany a police officer as part of the police ride alone program. Coincidentally, but not too coincidentally, it was participating in a police officer ride along program that caused Tommy Holt, Jr., the citizen, to immerse himself in the necessary empathy of walking in the shoes of police officers. My personal ride along experiences with veteran police officers was extensive and quite educational because my ride-along took place when I was yet a young college student who had just gotten out of the military and started working as a San Diego County Marshal. Subsequently, I went to work as a San Diego County Marshal within one month of getting discharged from the U.S. Navy. Looking back on those days of my brief stint in law enforcement, those were some of the more gut-wrenching and exciting days of my life. I'm proud I did it, and if I had to do it all over again, I would follow the same path. I will forever understand the eerie feelings that police officers feel each time they approach an unknown person, vehicle, and situation. Multiply those uneasy feelings for each time they approach a closed door, covered window, or occupied vehicles with an obstructed view.

There is a need for modern day society to funnel our youth through the ride along program as a prerequisite check off for high school graduation. A high school program comprised of the SLIP curriculum is an appropriate platform for providing an overarching umbrella to give youth the structure and maintenance of a pre-graduation ride-along program. The biggest payoff of such a program is, this type of program can save lives of citizens and police officers via educating. And who knows maybe how many curious and impressive young minds might choose a career and become law enforcement officers themselves?

Now, getting back to my recommendation to read the book called Black and Blue—here is why I recommend this book so highly. The author of Black and Blue happens to be a black man. While race is not a relevant factor in whether "Black and Blue" is a useful book for improving police and community relations, the fact that its author is a black man is an added bonus. How so? Obviously, the issues of race are front and center in the discussion of police and community relations. Actually, there is an automatic level of built in trust that comes with the messenger of "Black and Blue" that some writers coming from different backgrounds must work harder to buildup. Let's face it, non-minority police officers face low credibility in communities wherein the level of trust ranks between zero and two on a scale of one to ten, in terms of police and community relations.

Readers of color might establish a high level of comfort, although, at the same time, they might also feel a common sense of frustration early on in Black and Blue as the author shares a candidly personal experience of a high school step show. During that step show, he gets pepper sprayed by aggressive police officers. The author of Black and Blue was a teenager back then as some other people who attended the step show, that was supposed to be nothing more than a good night of carefree fun in a party atmosphere, chose to act like knuckleheads. The next thing the teenager, who grows up to become a SWAT officer knew, he and a group of other good youngsters found themselves burning like hell from a heavy dose of pepper spray. A few months later, the author, who was still a teenager, found himself on the receiving end of a blatant DWB case. In case you don't know, DWB stands for "driving while black or brown." The unique thing about this case of DWB is; not only was young Tommy Holt, Jr. subjected to the unwarranted harassment of racial profiling, the man that young Tommy regarded as his hero, then and now, his father, was the driver of the car.

Speaking of Tommy's father, I can't emphasize enough, how much, Tommy referred to his father as his hero. Tommy's father was not only a great dad and husband to the Holt family, but he was Tommy's football coach as well. As I digress, I can remember personally how truly grandiose the sport of football feels to a young man who is playing the sport while in high school. But sooner, rather than later, in Tommy's young adult life, Tommy grew to understand that although, his father and mentor, though, near perfect, did not obtain perfection of character. Tommy learned that his father, like so many other creatures of their environment, harbored an excessive level of mistrust and resentment towards the police. I will add, though, his father's ill feelings towards the police were not always accurate, those feelings were not totally without merit. The important thing is; Tommy was blessed with the open-mindedness to come to realize the era of his dear old dad's ways at a young age. That realization is significant, today more so than ever, given the climate of people who continue to harbor generational hate.

It is indeed Tommy's realization that good and bad, and right and wrong come in all forms, that makes Tommy a useful tool in the fight against police officers killing citizens and citizens killing police officers. Good and bad are not restricted or multiplied based on skin color. And likewise, it is not relevant based on the color of a uniform that people wear. We all should be so lucky to undergo that epiphany that Tommy was fortunate enough to receive. Tommy's evolution of not prejudging went on to serve himself, his community, and his whole country well. He had a brief but honorable military career, then he had a career in fire and rescue, which took him to the front lines of the tragedy of 911. Ultimately, he went on to serve gallantly in law enforcement and thereby rising to the level of SWAT officer. God only knows how many lives Officer Tommy saved or changed due to his ability to grow into racial maturity. When it comes to growing to an appropriate level of racial awareness, far too many people don't grow up today. Kudos to SWAT Officer Tommy for growing up and releasing the chains of narrow-mindedness and the blinders of bias thinking. We all should be so lucky because through shedding our racial bigotry, we become transformed into a person who can offer solutions rather than allowing bitterness to alter the trajectory of our lives and careers. Stumbling through life wearing blinders of bias thinking causes people to paint all police officers and specific segments of our society with a broad brush which says that all are bad, or all are good. That path is always a dangerous road to take.

My reasons for promoting SWAT Officer Tommy's book called, Black and Blue are multifaceted.

I hope you will come to understand and appreciate, his efforts and mine. One reason is, SWAT Officer Tommy is someone I can relate to. Just like me, he is an author who wrote a self-help book that aims to teach people how to see both sides of the community and police relations. I can't tell you how many books I read that are written by law enforcement officers who simply do not get it. This is not much of an exaggeration, 10 or 15 minutes into reading most books written by police officers, is enough to cause objective readers to roll their eyes and think, oh boy, here we go again. Time for the "pie in the sky" stories about the following types of propaganda: a) All police officers are always right. b) Police officers never tell lies. c) Police officers are 100% misunderstood in each and every situation, no matter how obvious the truth is to onlookers and outraged citizens. d) Police officers always have good intentions. e) Police officers never kill unarmed people for any other reasons, except for fear of losing their own lives. f) Police officers never harbor racial ill will towards people of color. g) Police officers never kill any unarmed people due to reckless disregard for human life based on the racial makeup or other discrimination. h) Police officers are always the true victim whenever they take human life. The list of enabling stereotypes goes on and on, but I'm sure, you get the message.

The point is; it is so refreshing to finally see a written testimonial from a decorated police officer who bares his soul and admits, that there are good and bad people on both sides of complex exchanges between police officers and citizens. And yes, it goes without saying, there are a great many people who fall somewhere in between the good and the bad too. It seems silly to have to write those last two sentences, but it never ceases to amaze that there are so many people who live in a fantasy world that says all police officers are good, or bad. Also absurd is the silly notion that all people that the police officers kill are good, or bad.

Here's a hint; SWAT Officer Tommy often segues into his life lessons by starting off the segments with the words "Truth Time." I don't want to play the spoiler, therefore, I'll let you read Officer

Tommy's dramatic story about how he got ambushed in a tight space and before he knew what was going on, he found himself locked in a fight for his life with a man who was high on a specific types of drugs, and in addition to that, the man had extraordinary martial arts skills, to boot. During Officer Tommy's fight from hell with the devil of a man, the man kept grabbing Officer Tommy's gun and saying, "I'm going to kill you!" I won't give away any more details, but let's suffice it to say: this story will give you chills and alter your breathing while you read it as the suspense unravels. The moral of the story is to give citizens a chance to say to themselves if this was you; would you shoot this unarmed man. Or how about; if this was your brother, your husband, or your dad or your son--would you want them to shoot this man and save their own life. Or would you just let the events play themselves out and hope that the asshole doesn't win the fight and kill you or your family member?

Having said all of the above positive things about SWAT Officer Tommy, I will use this time to say this; I am a person who formulates my opinions based on my personal experience and knowledge. I am not a person who follows the leader, or the herd, with blinders on--I make up my own mind. There are a number of points, opinions, and facts according to Officer Tommy's perspective that I do not agree with. For instance, I learned during the course of earning my Bachelor's Degree in Criminal Justice Administration, that statistically speaking, people of an alike race are by far more likely the ones who commit violent crimes against each other. Quick and basic research confirm the outcomes of such interactions via statistical data. It is no surprise, the people who surround us, interact with us the most. Obviously, they interact with us in good ways, but also, they interact with us in bad ways too. Reports from the FBI and other crime statistics bureaus directly conflict with SWAT Officer Tommy's theory about 82.5% of violent crimes against whites are perpetrated by blacks. In fact, the strangely over-the-top suggestion that blacks commit 82.5% of violent crimes against whites bares an eerie parallel to a notorious spreading of bad information that, then-candidate Trump, re-tweeted on November 2016. In that case, candidate Trump re-tweeted that blacks kill 81% of whites. Fact checkers quickly dispelled the data as a false report. Not only was the inaccuracy of the information, a product of fake news, but the so-called source of the news--Crime Statistics Bureau of San Francisco, did not exist. In fact, blacks kill 15% of whites, whites kill 8% of blacks, blacks kill 90% of blacks, and whites kill 82% of whites. Like I started out this conversation saying, people of alike race kill each other, most often. At the end of the day, one can always find room for disagreement among even more like-minded people, no matter how much they share common ideas, goals, and theories.

Another theory by SWAT Officer Tommy that I disagree with is his theory about the reason White police officers shoot black people so often. The theory goes, essentially, white police officers shoot blacks most frequently because 75% of police officers are white and only 25% of police officers are minorities. Doesn't that premise equate to this statement: most terrorists are Muslims because fewer non-Muslims are terrorists? The gist of the point is true, however, what's the point of giving credence to that message? Shouldn't we focus our attention on these relevant facts: 1) There are too many terrorists, 2) Terrorism is wrong, and 3) Terrorism is a problem that must be solved via zero tolerance policies? The same goes for excessive deadly force by police officers.

Another sticking point I have with SWAT Officer Tommy's book is; I want to see him use his platform to raise awareness and sensitivity, all across the board, by calling attention to the cold hard fact that police officers are taught to always shoot to kill, when and if, they shoot people. The shoot to kill philosophy is a cold, harsh reality that I learned in college back when I was earning my Bachelor's Degree in Criminal Justice Administration. The premise of killing a human being to eliminate red tape and personal inconvenience is outdated and inhumane. The time has come when some smart people should find a better way to resolve this problem.

The shoot to kill policy truly does sting all the way to hell and back, especially, when it turns out that the victim was unarmed in the first place--far too many times this turns out to be the case nowadays. Let's face it, families and legal opportunists are coming after the police officers that fire the shots, and his police department, anyway. So why not let the poor guy or gal live if it is at all possible to do so? The first step towards rectifying the shoot to kill problem is to create policies that eliminate the biggest motivating factors that cause police officers to shoot to kill. Sadly enough, but believe it or not, police officers shoot to kill as a matter of their own personal convenience. What personal convenience, you say? How about this convenience? When police officers shoot to kill, they instantly eliminate the victims' testimony and the lawsuits that the victims might bring against them. Remember, both the public and jurors might feel a deep sense of empathy towards the actual paralyzed, comatose, or bandaged from head to toe victims of police officer shootings if they are allowed to listen to and look into the weary eyes of said victims. In other words, dead men tell no tales. Why not keep it simple by creating laws to protect police officers, as well as, reassuring them with confidence that they are protected from all personal liability if their names are cleared of wrongdoing in a shooting or whatever line of duty killings they cause?

Finally, an issue of huge concern to me that SWAT Officer Tommy failed to address is the fact that mental illness is on the rise these days like never before, particularly autism spectrum disorders. Society needs to hear good active duty police officers talk about mental illness sensitivity procedures and budget allocations which are geared towards programs for educating police officers to humanely and safely deal with people with mental illness. Just as SWAT Officer Tommy puts it, "Perception is 90% of someone's reality. The truth exists in the remaining 10%." I am going on record right here and now: "The growing divide that exists between the mentally ill, and undertrained police officers, who sometimes are also unsympathetic, has our civilized society destined to collide head-on with an epidemic of police shootings of people with ASD and other mental illness issues." To make matters worse, not only are our police forces not equipped but more times than not, they show up thinking they have all the answers. Then the guns come out, and down goes a beloved person who, if handled differently, would still be alive. As Leonardo Da Vinci proclaimed so wisely, "The greatest deception men suffer is from their own opinions."

I'm a person who takes the time to read many of the books on policing that are on the market today. In my heart of hearts, as the saying goes; "In a million years,' I'll never understand why some of the tragedies of police officers killing citizens happen?" Like so many others, I find myself thinking, "Why did a person choose to take a human being's life rather than using the appropriate force needed to subdue and make the arrest. And due to the fact that I have a law enforcement background myself, I really don't get it. Adversely, I'll never understand when citizens randomly seek out and kill innocent police officers. Therefore, I'll keep reading with the hope that maybe little by little, I will get understanding. Most of the books I read are written by police officers. Many of such books offer useful information that I use as building blocks toward getting the understanding that I so crave. Likewise, most of such books are well-intentioned, but far too many times the books that I come across on police and community relations are written with both too much empathy for one side of the issues, and too little empathy for the other side. You know, it's like listening to a political conversation these days. All you here is, we are all good and they are all bad. Then of course, what's the next thing we do as readers of such books? We quickly get annoyed, and then we hastily tune out the conversation altogether. First of all, we don't like what the other side is saying. And second, we don't want to spend our valuable time listening to someone, who we perceive is a jerk, who chooses sit there put us down via condemnation of our beliefs. The end result is; it doesn't matter if the message is good or bad, the gist of the message gets lost.

The rare quality that makes SWAT Officer Tommy so unique is the fact that he takes an inclusive writing style instead of taking the redundantly overused "us vs them" approach that you often see used by anti-police and police worshipping writers. I really appreciate SWAT Officer Tommy's approach to writing Black and Blue because throughout the book he is relentless in his conviction that both sides can and need to do better. Black and Blue gives us examples,

theories, and workable solutions for building the bridge that is sorely

lacking. SWAT Officer Tommy gets it. He writes a section called,

"Perception is Reality." In that section, I am struck by the way he

opens up the section with these words, "I've found through my

experiences on both sides of the 'thin blue line' that each side has a

version of its own personal horror movie. It might not be real to you,

but it's real to them. At that specific moment in time, that person's

viewpoint is all that matters." That all ties into something I've said

before that's worth repeating, SWAT Officer Tommy's theory is that

perception is 90% of a person's reality, and the truth only exists in the

remaining 10% and more often than not, the reality is only seen after

it is too late. That being said, those out-of-whack variables and

constants are what led SWAT Officer Tommy to the following

conclusion: "If citizens find it within themselves to show sympathy for

what police officers are going through, they have a much higher

chance of survival."

Let's bring the focus of this discussion back to the survival of

the citizens. Survival of the citizens is what this book called SLIP is

all about. That is precisely my reason for recommending the book called Black and Blue, so highly. Both books, though, written by two entirely different men who never met before and who never knew about each other at the time of writing these books, share a common passion and desire to teach people how to survive each police encounter, no matter what the circumstances are. SLIP has a mantra, "SLIP Away from Harm." Black and Blue has a mantra; "Come Home SCHOOL."

When I created SLIP I was mindful to; keep-it-simple-stupid (KISS). Therefore, SLIP is very straightforward. SLIP stands for Stop and Listen to Instruction of the Police. If you follow that simple, but wise advice, you will pretty much survive any police encounter. I guarantee that. On the hand, Officer Tommy's SCHOOL is a bit more complex; however, the intent and the outcome are identical. If you don't get anything else from Black and Blue; be sure to get this: Officer Tommy says the biggest red flag citizens must recognize in order to know that they are in a situation wherein they or their group might lose their lives is when they see a police officer(s) acting aggressive. He said that citizens must recognize that the officer is in a state of fear himself. SWAT Officer Tommy then uses the word FEAR as an acronym, and he goes on to say, fear causes people to make mistakes, use bad judgement, and harm others in an effort to save themselves--no matter if the threat they perceive is real or not.

Now, let's talk about why SWAT Officer Tommy calls his system of saving lives via self-preservation methods, SCHOOL. The "S" in SCHOOL stands for Stop & show slow. The "C" stands for Communicate with a smile. "H" stands for Hold your ground. The first "O" in SCHOOL stands for Observe. The next "O" stands for Open a dialogue. The "L" stands for Live & learn. Needless to say, SCHOOL is excellent advice from a man who is exceptionally qualified to tell people what they should do whenever they are confronted by police officers.

I'm going to close this eye-opening chapter with a little discussion on a subject that makes SWAT Officer Tommy so uniquely qualified to create a system that works for all people. SWAT Officer Tommy Talks about his understanding of the dynamics of options vs. opportunity within the poorer communities. He proclaims, "What's the purpose of trying to explain to some of my white police colleagues that the reason why crime is so high in the 'black neighborhoods' isn't due to the amount of pigment in our skin?

Instead, it's due to the systematic, financial, political, social, and physical boundaries." The mere fact that SWAT Officer Tommy gets it, is enough to make me rally around him and support his cause of self-preservation. He is a man who places a strong emphasis on the importance of knowing the denotation of options vs opportunity. Options are the opportunity or ability to choose something or to choose between two or more things. In other words, options are something that can be chosen--a choice or possibility. Opportunity is an amount of time or a situation in which something can be done, or a favorable juncture of circumstances, a chance for advancement or progress. Anytime I have a privilege to come across a police officer that gets the fact that a huge reason for the skyrocketed crime rates in poor neighborhoods is a direct result of the correlation between the lack of options vs opportunity, I will tell as many people as I can: "Hey, come take a look at this guy, he is on to something special."

Whether you read SLIP first, and then read Black and Blue, doesn't matter so much. Just know this; you would make yourself much wiser if you read both books. Having written SLIP, I recognized right away that SCHOOL and SLIP, both mean the same thing, although they are two different acronyms. Both acronyms are a roadmap that leads to the same destination. However, SCHOOL was written by a seasoned and accomplished police officer. Therefore, SCHOOL is full of real-time hidden gems and practical nuggets such as: "If in DOUBT - lay it OUT." Which means, literally, "Maintain your hands up over your head and go into a kneeling position, one knee at a time. Then slowly bend at the waist with your hands still up until you are staring at the ground. Finally, place your hands on the ground in front of you slowly and walk your feet back until you are completely flat on the ground." Those kinds of details and insights, I was not able to offer as a person with very limited active duty law enforcement. But on the other hand, SLIP is written in such a way that the spirit of SLIP comes from a citizen's perspective because I am more able to step back and view police officers the way real people see them, though.

8 Gone but Not Forgotten

Those who cannot remember the past are condemned to repeat it, George Santayana, Poet and Philosopher.

Chapter eight is a brief look backwards at how much, or dare I say, how little police and community relations have changed over the past two decades. Not only that, chapter eight attempts to provide a snapshot into the two decades of evolution of the mindset of the author of SLIP. Hopefully, readers of SLIP can feel how much the author has grown wiser since writing 201 Reasons Not to Trust Police nearly two decades ago. I have come to learn that the highly volatile and always complex relationship between citizens and the police need people who are all about creating peace and harmony between the two sides. The last thing the minefields of police and citizen relations need is people who are clueless enough to think that either side is always right or wrong. Back when I wrote 201 Reasons Not to Trust Police I was not unlike too many other flabbergasted people who dare to speak on the issues of police and citizen relationships today. But now, I am here to own the fact that I was one of the clueless, and foolish people, who let my emotions take me in the opposite direction of where I needed to go and lead others. Like so many other frustrated, and often well-meaning people of today, I tried to bring about solutions via magnifying divisions. Remember the old saying: "two wrongs don't make a right?" That old saying is still true today. Having said all that, it is unfortunate, but painfully clear as we look back at a snapshot of the past two decades of police and citizen relations, somehow things are worse today than they were 20 years ago. No other way to say it, there has been too little growth and too much stagnation and erosion of police and citizen relations over the past two decades.

Speaking of looking back, about 20 years ago, this was one of the tragic stories that troubled me the most. 19-yr-old Tyisha Miller, a young black female, was shot 12 times by white and Hispanic police officers of the Riverside Police Department. She was shot as she laid in a parked car on December 28, 1998.

Tyisha's case struck a nerve with me back then because I had a young daughter that I couldn't begin to imagine how I could carry on if something so senseless and tragic happened to her. Like most fathers in the world, I loved my little girl more than life itself. As such, I couldn't even imagine how Tyisha Miller's parents managed to carry on after she was shot and killed in what felt like an execution-style murder.

I remember having a heart to heart conversation with a wise old friend who was a veteran survivor of two major wars--the Vietnam War and the Korean War. He was a highly decorated senior enlisted man of war. I told him it would be a struggle for me to stay on the right side of the law, if such an awful tragedy as the what happened to Tyisha Miller, happens to a family member of mine. Remember, this was me talking, back when I was 20 years younger. Of course, the years have softened my edges and lowered my testosterone.

The old war hero I was talking to, looked me in the eyes and said, with a serious tone of voice that caused me to feel the power of his passion. He uttered these words: "If the police killed my family member that way, I would get one of them to revenge the death of my loved one." He went on to say: "I'm as good with weapons as anybody, so I'll be damned if I wouldn't choose a time and a place that I can take out one of theirs."

My question to him was, "Are you saying you would kill a random police officer?" "Yea, if they take out one of mine, I'd take out one of theirs. Doesn't have to be the ones who killed mine. They are a brotherhood, so I'd take out one of their brothers. That will remind them that, number one; there are consequences for killing innocent people even though the courts never punish them. Number two; I'll make damn sure they feel how bad it feels to lose someone you care about for no legitimate reason."

That conversation is seared into my brain, because now more than ever, there is a lesson of life to be learned in that way of thinking. The lesson to be learned is of significant relevance to people in law enforcement. For disclosure, the man who uttered those words about getting revenge for his family member's wrongful death was not a "whack job." He was a very patriotic, very distinguished and highly decorated career military man. My take away from that conversation is this; those who are tasked with standing before a room full of police officers to advise them should compel those police officers to think about the big picture. The big picture is; before police officers act too hastily and take the lives of citizens whenever other options are on the table, don't do it. The point is, although, sometimes taking human life is the proper option, good police officers must act with a preference for using non-lethal methods first.

Cameras are recording your actions and social media are retelling the story of your life taking action over and over again. Remember, social media provides a platform, for people who forward images of your actions, to add their own dramatic twist. Those dramatic twists on what happened becomes reality. Often those videos and the social media spin of your devious deeds go viral and thereby becomes fuel for retaliation by disturbed, angry, bitter, or radicalized individuals.

The big picture is, police officers should act with caution before taking human life unless it is the last resort, because the life you save, might be your own. Or you might save the lives of other good police officers who are doing things the right way. Good police officers can get murdered just because they find themselves in the wrong place at the wrong time, as they come face to face with an angry revenge-minded person. Today, those words are not theory, those words are fact.

In the case of Tyisha Miller, the police officers that shot the teenager claimed that they shot her when she lunged for a gun. However, a witness on the scene said that the teenager was having a seizure. So she was incapacitated and unarmed. Riverside is a city that is about 60 miles east of Los Angeles, CA. The incident has sparked protests, but not nearly enough to move the national needle.

Ultimately, a report filed via Grand Jury investigation of the Tyisha Miller case came across with a tone which suggested that the police officers of the Riverside Police Department were the real victims. And in the end, the Grand Jury did not recommend charging police officers with any wrongdoings, instead, it recommended the department hire more cops, conduct better training, and implement a discipline review panel.

Sorting through the police officers' explanations for their actions in Tyisha Miller's case, her family walked away feeling like the Riverside Police Officers, pretty much said: "Oops… My bad, but it was her fault!" Given the fact that a promising life was cut short in a horrific manner, that is a damn shame.

A relative of Tyisha Miller told a source that she called the police for assistance because of her cousin, the late deceased youngster, was locked inside her car having a seizure. The cousin called with the hope of getting medical assistance for Tyisha Miller. Instead, when the police officers arrived on the scene and saw a gun in the 19-year-old's car, they panicked and began over-reacting as they approached the car from different angles.

A police officer at the front driver side of the car accidentally dropped his nightstick on the parking lot pavement, the noise from the fallen nightstick caused the police officer at the rear of the car on the opposite side to think that gunshots were being fired. This caused the overly anxious cops to enter a state of chaos and within a few seconds, Tyisha Miller's body and the car were riddled with bullets.

Looking at this tragic incident in hindsight, I'm sure that if young, inexperienced Tyisha had the opportunity to relive that scenario, she would have made sure that the gun in the car was completely out of sight.

The criminal justice system should mandate standard protocol for police officers regarding shots fired. Specifics should be in place, based on whether a suspect attempts to raise a firearm or points a gun at other human beings. Each state should have pre-set guidelines that cover the officers from liability in case of accidental shootings. By doing so, officers will or maybe, less likely to shoot to kill and more likely to tell the truth about the shooting.

Instead, under present conditions police officers who are accused of wrongful shootings are exonerated by an ancient criminal justice process known as compurgation. Just like in the early days of a primitive criminal justice system, even though people are known to assemble a number of their peers who will take an oath and validate their innocence, the system is not showing any signs of changing.

Another notorious case of police officers jumping the gun and shooting an unarmed man that happened 20-years-ago was that of Amadou Diallo. Under most circumstances, who can remember the details of such a distant tragedy? Yet, under certain other circumstances, who can forget the surreal, over the top way, young Amadou Diallo's life was taken? When I close my eyes and allow myself to be a spider on the wall watching the tragedy unfold during that horrific incident, I feel like I'm watching an old war movie in which, the American heroes take out an alien enemy of the state. But just for one moment, stop and let yourself imagine what emotions Amadou Diallo's family must still feel when they close their eyes and imagine what their dearly departed loved one's last minute on this earth was like.

Newspapers in black communities read something like this: "Four white police officers fired 41 shots at an unarmed black man in the Bronx, NY in February of 1999. The man was shot 19 times. Once again, the American Justice System, that is far too soft on police crimes, vindicated the four police officers. A jury in Albany, NY found the four white police officers, innocent of all charges in Diallo's killing on February 25, 2000."

When you cut to the chase, the defense of the four police officers was: "Oops… My bad, Mr Diallo was holding a wallet in his hand, not a gun – we all thought his wallet was a gun." My reaction back then was simply, "Excuse me. But what did you say?"

I struggled to wrap my brain around that whole scenario. I felt like, "Oh man, if the police officers are that stupid in New York, I am glad that I live in California." I remember thinking such thoughts back then when the explanation for exonerating those four trigger-happy police officers came out in the press, nearly 20 years ago. A peculiar thing is, I can still see the images in my mind of a police officer shedding "crocodile" tears while testifying under oath in that case.

Speaking of old cases that will never die in terms of relevance, although, this particular case is nearly 20-years-old, as well. This is a case that I mentioned multiple times throughout SLIP. There are several reasons for that, but most of all, the DuBose case inspired me to write on the complex topic of police and citizen relations.

The specifics of the case are, on July 24, 1999, two San Diego Police Officers shot former Notre Dame Star and Tampa Bay Buccaneers linebacker, 12 to 15 times – depending on whose report you believe, including five shots in his back. The rest of the bullets entered his torso, in the general vicinity of his heart--most of those shots entered the left side of his back. The justice system declared that the two police officers who shot 28-year-old Adolphus D. DuBose were just doing their jobs.

The police were called because Mr DuBose had been partying and gotten too buzzed, then accidentally entered a neighbor's residence and went to sleep–he thought he was home. Naturally, when the resident discovered him, he was cautious and called 911. But when the police officers arrived the matter was cleared up to the resident's satisfaction. This was a matter of a confused man in a confusing situation. No harm intended, no harm done. However, according to witnesses, the two police officers would not let it go.

In a nutshell, the two police officers wanted to put handcuffs on DuBose but he expressed to the cops that handcuffs were totally unnecessary. This terribly wrong choice of judgement by DuBose marked the beginning of the end for DuBose. Naturally, the two police officers did not agree with DuBose. Witnesses said at that time DuBose got up from sitting on the stairs, against police officers' orders, and started to walk away in a nonchalant manner. So one of the two police officers jumped on DuBose's back and was easily thrown off. Then the two police officers set out to arrest DuBose. But it had to be clear to all onlookers, God, and the two police officers involved, that those two police officers were not men enough to subdue Mr DuBose, who at that point had proven that he had no intentions of being arrested by the two police officers. Of course, that was a terribly wrong decision by DuBose. The police officers then attacked with nunchucks and pepper spray but claimed that they still could not handle DuBose.

Even if you are not a police officer and have never been to the police academy, I'll bet you know what the police officers should do next, don't you? I'm pretty sure you have enough common sense and have seen enough television and movies, to know that this is the point where any police officer worth a penny of taxpayer's money, takes a few seconds and calls for backup, right? Right! After all, the police officers were dealing with a man that was making little or no effort to flee, so they had time to call for backup, and simply wait for backup to arrive.

Next, comes the point wherein video footage would have yielded huge benefits toward clearing up confusion surrounding the D.A.s office primary defense evidence for the two police officers. Of course, the accused police officers were quick to say that DuBose had a police officer's nunchucks in his hands.

One thing that is very suspect, is the question of whether DuBose lunged at the police officers or not with the nunchucks. Video footage could have made a world of difference in getting to the bottom of that crucial question. However, in reality, surely the officers would have been cleared of all charges in that case, anyway, no matter what.

The statistics suggest officers are pretty much always cleared in such officer-involved shootings. But we all know one thing for certain, when a man truly lunges at a police officer with a weapon, there are no questions as to whether the man truly lunged at him or not. In the absence of video proof to contradict the officers' testimony, we will never know whether DuBose lunged at the officers with the nunchucks or not.

Let's look at the situation realistically. If a man takes a defensive posture, or even slightly lunges towards any two people with nunchucks, can these two people shoot him 12 times, including five times in the back and get away with it? Of course, logic and common sense say the answer to that question is, no.

To show how truly ridiculous this shooting was, this whole physical confrontation took place outdoors. The police officers had plenty space and opportunity to move around freely and keep themselves safe while backups arrived to reinforce their situation. In other words, the shooting excuse used by the police officers would have had some merit if the police officers could say, "We were cornered by the suspect or we felt cornered that there was nothing also we could do to protect ourselves or nearby civilians."

San Diego District Attorney's Office ruled that no criminal

charges be brought against the two police officers that shot Mr DuBose 12 times. Less than one year after the DuBose shooting that same San Diego District Attorney's Office came under criticism and investigations which led to convictions of multiple counts of misconduct, including cover-ups!

When police officers have the option to call for backup rather than take human life, the criminal justice system should mandate that backup is called, as well as, alternative policing techniques must be utilized whenever possible. After all, we do not live under the inquisitorial system of justice, wherein the accused is guilty until proven innocent. Instead, we live under the adversary system, wherein people are innocent until proven guilty.

The DuBose case is a textbook example of why I wrote "SLIP." At the heart of everything that "SLIP" stands for is spreading this message: citizens must, "Always cooperate, never resist!" After all, the life we save might be our own.

In conclusion, true wisdom dictates the following simple actions by both, the communities and the police departments: 1)

People need to talk, and listen to each other about finding workable solutions. 2) And at the same time, people should keep these words in mind, "Blessed are the peacemakers: for they shall be called the children of God." Matthew 5:9